Biblical Women

Kaleidoscope

Statement of Purpose

Kaleidoscope is a series of adult educational resources developed for the ecumenical church by Lancaster Theological Seminary and the United Church Board for Homeland Ministries. Developed for adults who want serious study and dialogue on contemporary issues of Christian faith and life, Kaleidoscope offers elective resources designed to provide new knowledge and new understanding for persons who seek personal growth and a deeper sense of social responsibility in their lives.

Kaleidoscope utilizes the expertise of professionals in various disciplines to develop study resources in both print and video. The series also provides tools to help persons develop skills in studying, reflecting, inquiring critically, and exploring avenues of appropriate Christian responses in life.

Kaleidoscope provides sound and tested resources in theology, biblical studies, ethics, and other related subjects that link personal growth and social responsibility to life situations in which adult Christian persons develop.

Biblical Women

Mirrors, Models, and Metaphors

Elizabeth Huwiler

*Combined Leader's Guide and
Student Edition*

A Kaleidoscope Series Resource

United Church Press
Cleveland, Ohio

KALEIDOSCOPE SERIES

United Church Press, Cleveland, Ohio 44115
© 1993 by United Church Press

Biblical quotations are from the New Revised Standard Version of the Bible,
© 1989 by the Division of Christian Education of the National Council of the
Churches of Christ in the U.S.A., and are used by permission

All rights reserved. Published 1993

Printed in the United States of America
The paper used in this publication is acid free and meets the minimum require-
ments of American National Standard for Information Sciences-Permanence of
Paper for Printed Library Materials, ANSI Z39.48-1984

98 97 96 95 94 93   5 4 3 2 1

Library of Congress Cataloging-in-Publication Data

Huwiler, Elizabeth, 1952-
        Biblical women : mirrors, models, and metaphors / Elizabeth Huwiler. —
combined leader's guide and student ed.
        p. cm. — (A Kaleidoscope series resource)
        Includes bibliographical references.
        ISBN 0-8298-0823-X (alk. paper)
        1. Women in the Bible. I. Title. II. Series.
BS575.H89 1993
220.9'2'082—dc20   93-6917
                                                                    CIP

Contents

Introduction to the Kaleidoscope Series

Through direct experience, our faculty at Lancaster Theological Seminary discovered that a continual demand exists for Christian theological reflection upon issues of current interest. To meet this demand, the seminary for many years has offered courses for lay people. To offer the substance of these courses to the wider Christian public is the purpose of the Kaleidoscope Series.

Lancaster Seminary exists to proclaim the gospel of Jesus Christ for the sake of the church and the world. In addition to preparing men and women for the ordained Christian ministry, the seminary seeks to be a center of theological reflection for clergy and laity. Continuing education and leadership development for all Christians focus our mission. The topics and educational style in the Kaleidoscope Series extend Lancaster Seminary's commitment: theological study reflective of the interaction of the Bible, the world, the church, worship, and personal faith. We hope that this course will provide an opportunity for you to grow in self-understanding, in knowledge of other people and God's creation, and in the spirit of Christ.

We wish to thank the current and former staff of the Division of Education and Publication of the United Church Board for Homeland Ministries for their leadership in this enterprise. The Reverend Ansley Coe Throckmorton, the Reverend Dr. Larry E. Kalp, and the late Reverend Dr. Percel O. Alston provided encouragement and support for the project. In particular, we are grateful for the inspiration of Percel Alston, who was a trustee of Lancaster Seminary. His lifelong interest in adult education makes it most appropriate that this series be dedicated to him. Finally, I wish to recognize the creative leadership of Mrs. Jean Vieth, the seminary coordinator for the series, who has been active for several years in this educational program at Lancaster.

Peter M. Schmiechen, President
Lancaster Theological Seminary

How to Use the Kaleidoscope Series

The Kaleidoscope book is the basic resource for all students in the Kaleidoscope Series. Bound into the back of each Kaleidoscope book is a Leader's Guide, and the leader will need to study both the text and the Leader's Guide to prepare to lead study sessions. The accompanying video is a very helpful tool for the class using this book as a study resource.

Other KALEIDOSCOPE resources are

- *BECOMING PEOPLE OF THE WAY: Intentional Christianity,* by Francis Ringer
- *BREAD FOR THE BANQUET: Experiencing Life in the Spirit,* by Elaine M. Ward
- *THE GIFT AND THE PROMISE: Becoming What We Are in Christ,* by Peter Schmiechen
- *GOD, WHERE ARE YOU? Suffering and Faith,* by Richard F. Vieth
- *INTIMACY: The Quest for Life Connections,* by James W. Hanna
- *JOURNEY THROUGH THE PSALMS: A Path to Wholeness,* by Denise Dombkowski Hopkins
- *NOBODY'S CHILD: A Generation Caught in the Middle,* by Paul E. Irion
- *PASS IT ON: Telling and Hearing Stories from John,* by Gilbert Bartholomew
- *STRETCH OUT YOUR HAND: Exploring Healing Prayer,* by Tilda Norberg and Robert D. Webber
- *THUNDER ON THE RIGHT: Understanding Conservative Christianity,* by Elizabeth C. Nordbeck

Introduction

Welcome to a study of biblical women.

This book has two identities. On the one hand, it is a book about biblical women. Each chapter has a specific content: women's roles in biblical times; women relating to other women; women relating to men; women relating to Jesus; women in two famous texts involving gardens (Eden and the Song of Songs); and gender and God. So in each chapter you will have an opportunity to learn something about women's identities and relationships in the Bible.

On the other hand, this is a book about interpreting biblical texts that relate to women. Each chapter has not only a content but also a method: historical reconstruction; dynamic analogy; hermeneutic of suspicion; reading from below; interpreting the tradition; constructive biblical theology. So in each chapter you will also be able to learn a way of approaching biblical texts. Once you become familiar with these methods, you will be able to apply them to other biblical texts and thus enrich your own reading of the Bible—whether as an individual, in your family, or in a study group.

Who are biblical women? There are far too many of them to discuss in this book. I suspect that you will find some here that you already know well, and others may be new to you.

People today can approach biblical women in many different ways. The subtitle of this book labels three of these ways: mirrors, models, and metaphors. Biblical women can function as *mirrors*. We may see in their stories reflections of our own lives or the lives of women we know. Some of our own hopes and fears may be realized in the stories of long ago.

At other times we may look to biblical women as *models*. We may admire some of them so much that we want to conform our lives to theirs. Or, we may disapprove of them so heartily that we want to shape our lives in contrast to theirs. Thus, they may be either positive or negative models.

Some biblical women have functioned as *metaphors* for what it means to be a woman. Their stories have symbolized what our culture has told us is our identity or character or fate. At other times, the experiences of biblical women have become metaphors for experiences common to women in different eras. In addition, we will survey images of women and their lives that have functioned as metaphors for the divine.

I write this book as a Christian woman scholar, and in doing so I have two hopes. First, I hope that it reflects all the aspects of that identity—Christian, woman, and scholar. And second, I hope that it is useful not only to people who share that identity. I try throughout to be honest about my own interest in and attitudes toward these women and their stories. But in doing so I am not trying to suggest that you must approach them and appreciate them in the same way I do. Rather, it is my hope that by expressing my own opinions clearly, I will also open up the possibility for you to express your own acceptance of the stories into your own faith and life.

Chapter One

Women's Roles

Historical Reconstruction

What were women's roles in biblical times? They varied, of course. It is tempting for people in our culture to read recent history and assumptions back into biblical times. We might suppose that women were primarily perceived in relationship to men (their fathers, husbands, and sons) and that nothing else about a woman really mattered. It has even been suggested that the "single most important achievement of any biblical woman was to produce children, especially males."[1]

One way to test such assumptions is to check them against biblical texts. We might ask ourselves: how does the text present its women characters? How does it support our assumptions about biblical women? How does it qualify or even overturn them? We may be surprised. Consider the following text, which is from a narrative about finding a law scroll during the reign of King Josiah of Judah (639–609 B.C.E.):

> The high priest Hilkiah said to Shaphan the secretary, "I have found the book of the law in the house of Yahweh." When Hilkiah gave to book to Shaphan, he read it. Then Shaphan the secretary came to the king, and reported to the king, "Your servants have emptied out the money that was found in the house, and have delivered it into the hand of the workers who have oversight of the house of Yahweh." Shaphan the secretary informed the king, "The priest Hilkiah has given me a book." Shaphan then read it aloud to the king.
>
> When the king heard the words of the book of the law, he tore his clothes. Then the king commanded the priest Hilkiah, Ahikam son of Shaphan, Achbor son of Micaiah, Shaphan the secretary, and the king's servant Asaiah, saying, "Go, inquire of Yahweh for me, for the people, and for all Judah, concerning the words of this book that has been found; for great is the wrath of Yahweh that is kindled against us, because our ancestors did not obey the words of this book, to do according to all that is written concerning us."

> So the priest Hilkiah, Ahikam, Achbor, Shaphan, and Asaiah went to the prophetess Huldah the wife of Shallum son of Tikvah, son of Harhas, keeper of the wardrobe; she resided in Jerusalem in the Second Quarter, where they consulted her. She declared to them, "Thus says Yahweh, the God of Israel: Tell the man who sent you to me, Thus says Yahweh, I will indeed bring disaster on this place and on its inhabitants—all the words of the book that the king of Judah has read. Because they have abandoned me and have made offerings to other gods, so that they have provoked me to anger with all the work of their hands, therefore my wrath will be kindled against this place, and it will not be quenched. But as to the king of Judah, who sent you to inquire of Yahweh, thus shall you say to him, Thus says Yahweh, the God of Israel: Regarding the words that you have heard, because your heart was penitent, and you humbled yourself before Yahweh, when you heard how I spoke against this place, and against its inhabitants, that they should become a desolation and a curse, and because you have torn your clothes and wept before me, I also have heard you, says Yahweh. Therefore, I will gather you to your ancestors and you shall be gathered to your grave in peace; your eyes shall not see all the disaster that I will bring on this place." They took the message back to the king. (2 Kings 22:8-20)[2]

In this text, a scroll which appears to be significant has been found. The king send agents to authenticate the scroll and learn how it applies to the current situation. They go to Huldah the prophet, and she transmits to them the word of Yahweh.

Certainly the text supports some traditional assumptions about gender roles in ancient Israel and Judah. The king, of course, is a man, and so are all the officials sent to Huldah. Huldah is identified not only by her specific role (prophet) but also by her relationships with men (her husband, father-in-law, and grandfather-in-law).

The text also offers some surprises. The first is that the prophet is a woman. The second is that the prophet's sex is apparently not remarkable. The king needs to know the authenticity and importance of the scroll; he needs a prophet; the agents go to Huldah. They do not say, "We can't find a regular prophet, so we'll settle for a woman." Nor do they refer to Huldah as "a tolerable prophet even though she is a woman." Rather, it is simply "Huldah, the prophet." If we think that biblical women are important only for childbearing, we are surprised that the text does not bother to tell us whether Huldah is a mother.

Of course, this is an unusual text: there are many more that describe women only within family roles. But texts such as this give us the chance to see biblical women in a wider variety of roles than we might have expected.

Changing Roles and Status

When we speak of traditional women's roles, we may think of what has been traditional in our own society. Looking back in time, we may suppose that things have always been the same, only more so. If our mothers' and grandmothers' lives look restricted to us, how much more must biblical women have been restricted, living at a time when (we might suppose) a woman had no recognized existence apart from the men to whom she related as daughter or wife. We might guess that those men could demand absolute obedience, or even that the woman was legally her father's or husband's personal property. Such a woman could not have had any respect within her society. How could she have survived without suffocating?

But this scenario is not necessarily accurate. Women's roles a generation ago—or even several generations ago—cannot be read back into biblical times. First, although men's and women's roles were different in ancient societies, neither those differences nor the respect accorded sex roles was the same as today. In our society, work outside the home often provides higher status than work within the home. But during much of ancient Israel's history, the extended family was the society's basic unit of economic production, and virtually everyone, male and female, worked from the home.

Second, the idea of women as property is only partially accurate. In most ways, women were treated as persons in biblical law, and we see them acting as persons in narratives. What was male property was not the woman herself but control of her sexuality.[3] We may find it unthinkable that even a woman's sexuality could be male property, but to assume that this meant her whole self belonged to a man is to reduce that woman to her sexual function.

Third, the roles available to women and the status accorded them varied markedly during the thousands of years we refer to as the biblical period. We may distinguish the following eras:

The Time of the Ancestors. This is a period not of Israelites but of Israelite ancestors: Abraham and Sarah; Rebekah and Isaac; Jacob,

Leah, and Rachel. It is impossible for historians to reconstruct the lives of the ancestors with any certainty because the texts date from much later periods. Some scholars doubt that there is any historical validity at all to the ancestral narratives, while others find them on the whole convincing. The basic economic, legal, and religious unit in these texts is the extended family.

Egypt, Exodus, Torah, and Wilderness. During this time, Moses, Miriam, and Aaron are key figures. Again, historical documentation is impossible. When the later tradition looks back to the events that brought Israel together as a people, they sometimes speak of the Exodus from Egypt and sometimes of the giving of the Torah. The later tradition appears to combine a number of distinct memories of pre-Israelite groups.

Settlement and Pre-Monarchic Israel. The key settlement character in the biblical texts is Joshua. Pre-monarchic Israel is led by figures traditionally known as "judges," who hold various political and military roles. It is during this time that the Israelites begin to appear as a people. This is the time of the first documented external reference to Israel.[4]

Pre-monarchic Israelite society is basically agrarian. The extended family (usually called the "father's house") is the primary social unit. The Israelites live at a subsistence level. There is strong influence from Canaanite groups, which have a city-state organization.

Monarchic Israel and Judah. With royalty comes an increase in both urban population and specialized occupations. The royal court needs advisers, and recordkeepers. Royal ideas of national security require military leaders and at times a standing army. It is possible that literacy is especially connected with government scribes. Kings conscript residents for both military and domestic projects. Iron-age technology also requires more specialized metalworkers.

For most of this period (from about 900 B.C.E. on), the Israelites are divided into two realms, Israel in the north and Judah in the south. The two realms develop different traditions. Jerusalem with its temple and the Davidic dynasty belongs to the southern realm and may have little impact on the society or religion of the north. Northerners, on the other hand, may preserve a stronger tradition of Yahweh as the true ruler, charismatic (spirit-chosen) leaders, and less centralized worship. Prophecy, too, may be different in the two

realms, with southern prophets more likely to be officially connected with the royal court and northern prophets more likely to
stand in opposition to the political establishment.[5]

Israel, the northern realm, is conquered by the Assyrians in 722
B.C.E. Many northern refugees flee to the southern realm, increasing
its urbanization and providing for northern traditions to be
included in the life and literature of Judah. It is during this period,
after the destruction of the northern realm but before the demise of
Judah, that the story of Huldah belongs. Judah survives until the
Babylonian conquest of the early sixth century, when several large-
scale deportations (the largest in 597 and 587) send leading
Judahites (including the prophets Jeremiah and Ezekiel) into exile.
Many other residents remain behind.

Babylonian Exile. Although there are exilic communities in Egypt as
well as Babylon, the latter group is central in shaping earlier
traditions into what will become the Bible. It is likely that during
this period the form of the Pentateuch (Genesis through
Deuteronomy) becomes fixed, the historical books (or former
prophets: Joshua, Judges, Samuel, and Kings) are edited, and
memories of prophetic sayings are recorded to form the cores of
prophetic books such as Amos, Hosea, and Micah. Other books
(Psalms, for example) remain more fluid, and some (such as Esther,
Daniel, Ezra, and Nehemiah) have not yet been written.

Resettlement. Under Cyrus of Persia, beginning in 539 B.C.E., exiled
Judahites are allowed to return and rejoin those who had remained
behind in the conquered land. During this period, as in the first
settlement period, existence is at a subsistence level.

Second Temple Period. The reconstruction of the temple begins in
521 B.C.E. The rebuilt temple survives until 70 C.E., with another
major building period under Herod the Great (at about the time of
Jesus). This includes times of Persian, Greek, and Roman domination. During this time, most of the books of the Hebrew Bible
probably receive their final shaping, and ancient Israelite religion
begins to evolve into Judaism. The second temple period includes
the time of Jesus and the beginnings of the Christian church,
although most of the New Testament documents date from after
the destruction of the temple.

Relating Status to Historical Changes

The dynamics of gender relationships vary considerably through these diverse periods of Israelite, early Jewish, and early Christian history. Carol Meyers, a biblical scholar and archaeologist, has correlated sociological and anthropological studies of women's status with biblical and archaeological evidence about Israelite society during the various stages of its history.[6] First, she notes that women's status is generally highest when they contribute about 40 percent to the overall economic production of a society; she suggests that this is the percentage likely during the pre-monarchic and resettlement periods.[7]

Second, childbearing and the care of young children often keep women closely tied to the private sphere. When, as during agrarian periods, the family is also the basic economic unit, women's contributions are most likely to be recognized. In a more specialized society (such as developed in Jerusalem during the monarchy), in which the typical male workplace is not the household, it is easier for men to overlook or discount women's contributions.

Third, the attitudes of surrounding cultures have an impact on status. Meyers emphasizes this external influence during the Greek and Roman periods. She believes that Greek and Roman prejudices and legal limitations affected the status of Israelite and early Jewish and Christian women as well.

If she is correct, women may have enjoyed relatively high status in Israelite society during the pre-monarchic period. During the monarchy, respect for women may have declined as more men worked outside the household and at least some lived above the subsistence level. Under the renewed pioneer conditions of the resettlement period, women's status would have increased again, only to decline under Greek and Roman influence, which combined increasing urbanization and specialization with social prejudices and legal limitations on women.

This analysis is not always easy to apply to specific biblical texts. Several different historical periods may be relevant to a text: the time the text describes, the time it was first composed, and the time it reached its final form. Unfortunately for women's history, the major periods of literary activity may have been the monarchy, the Babylonian exile, and the Roman empire. Thus, biblical texts are likely to describe times when women's status was lowest.

This is not to suggest that authors and editors deliberately eliminated women's stories or limited women's significance in the stories they did include. But it is likely that their perceptions were so shaped by growing male domination and ideology that they could not see the importance of stories about women or the significance of women's roles in the stories in which women did play a part.

Thus it becomes all the more important to look for a text's surprises, to note where we find women in roles we didn't know they could play. We may find behind the texts an implication that women had more authority over their own lives and more significance in society than later keepers of the tradition want to admit.

Family Roles

The most common women's roles, in the Bible as in all times, are within the family. Although these roles are significant in defining a woman's place, they do not entirely determine her significance within either Israelite society or the Bible. There are women characters in biblical stories whose family relationships are not revealed in the text. Obviously, for those who shaped and transmitted their stories, family relationships did not give the most important information about these women.

Judith Romney Wegner determines six categories of free women in the Bible.[8] (In addition, we might note slave women, whose specific roles would be assigned by their owners.) Free women may be divided into dependent and independent, with three roles in each category. Dependent women include minor daughter (dependent on father), wife (dependent on husband), and levirate widow (dependent on husband's family).[9] The corresponding independent women are adult daughter, divorcée, and non-levirate widow.[10]

Most of this section is devoted to the matriarchs, paradigmatic wives and mothers. In the tradition, Sarah and Rebekah are understood as mothers of all Israel, and between them Leah and Rachel are presented as physical or legal mothers of all the Israelite tribes.

The Matriarchs

The matriarchs, women considered ancestors of Israel as a whole, include Sarah (wife of Abraham, Gen. 12-23), Rebekah (wife of Isaac, Gen. 24-27), and Leah and Rachel (wives of Jacob, Gen. 29-35). Hagar (Gen. 16 and 21) is not included. A servant of Sarah and secondary wife of Abraham, she is remembered not as a mother of Israel but as an ancestor of the Hebrews' Arab neighbors.[11] Nor is Keturah (Gen. 25), Abraham's wife after the death of Sarah, counted among the ancestors of Israel. Even Bilhah and Zilpah (Gen. 30-33), servants of Rachel and Leah and secondary wives of Jacob, are rarely remembered in the tradition, although they are acknowledged as ancestors of the tribes of Dan, Naphtali, Gad, and Asher. The tradition has forgotten all but their names. They were servants, not fully counted as wives.

Other women from the ancestral period who are not considered Israelite matriarchs include the unnamed women of Lot's household. His wife is identified in the tradition with the great salt pillars of the Dead Sea area (Gen. 19:26). Lot's two daughters, who believed that the destruction of Sodom and Gomorrah was worldwide (thus leaving only themselves and their father to perpetuate the human race), are remembered as the incestuous mothers of two neighboring groups, the Moabites and Ammonites (Gen. 19:38-38).

It is not realistic to devalue the matriarchs for being known primarily because of the children they bore. Aside from the fact that childbearing is a productive role in any society, these women are, after all, characters in ancestor stories. In these narratives, all the major characters, men as well as women, are known as parents. Sarah might well not be in the tradition if she were not remembered as an ancestor of the people of Israel—but the same is certainly true of Isaac.

Both Jews and Christians have traditionally referred to the ancestor stories as "patriarchal narratives."[12] This label directs interpreters to focus on the men in the stories and ignore the women. The texts themselves do not have any such title and, although more space is devoted to the men than to the women, some of the most interesting ancestor stories are about the mothers of Israel.

Sarah, the wife of Abraham, is the first of the matriarchs. When she first appears in the text (12:5), she does so simply as a member of the household of Abraham as he leaves his ancestral home for the land that Yahweh will show him. The cycle of stories about Sarah includes a deception of the Egyptian pharaoh, in which she is presented as Abraham's sister instead of his wife (12:10-20); her complicated relationship with Hagar, including persuading Abraham to try to have a child by Hagar and then rejecting Hagar and the child after the scheme succeeds (chapters 16 and 21); Yahweh's assurance to Abraham that the promise of progeny is through Sarah (17:15-22); the encounter with three visitors (18:1-15); a deception of King Abimelech, which parallels that of the Pharaoh (20:1-18); the birth of Isaac (21:1-18); and Sarah's death and burial (23:1-2, 19-20).

The primary tension in this cycle is between Yahweh's promise of a great nation of descendants and the fact that Abraham and Sarah have no children throughout their normal childbearing years. This childlessness leads to Hagar's role as surrogate mother and Sarah's later rejection of her. At the apparently ludicrous promise that Sarah would bear a child, first Abraham (17:17) and then Sarah (18:12-15) laugh. But only a few chapters later, when Sarah gives birth to Isaac, the laughter of derision is transformed into that of joy (21:6).

The stories about Sarah employ a spare narrative style that leaves undetermined the extent of both her autonomy and her authority over others. Did she share Abraham's belief that he had been called out of Ur to a new land (Gen. 12)? Was she a willing collaborator in the deceptions of the pharaoh and Abimelech, or did Abraham coerce her into presenting herself to these foreign kings as an unmarried woman? The text fails to mention Sarah at all in the story of Abraham's near-sacrifice of Isaac (Gen. 22). It is an entirely open question whether she even knew what Abraham expected to do and, if so, whether she fought his determination or agreed with it.

On two occasions, Sarah does instigate action involving Abraham and Hagar. First, she initiates the plan to make Hagar a surrogate mother, but there is no indication that Abraham objects to her idea. She also comes up with the idea to expel Hagar and Ishmael from the household. Abraham is troubled at her suggestion and does not follow through until Yahweh directs him to do so. Is his eventual acquiescence because Sarah has the authority to make the decision or because she happens to want something that accords with the divine will? The text is open to both readings.

Rebekah is the second of the matriarchs. There are only four stories about her, fewer than about any of the other matriarchs. Even so, she overshadows her husband, Isaac, who is not the hero of a cycle of stories as are his father and son.[13] Rebekah is an active character in three of the four stories that mention her: her engagement to Isaac arranged through Abraham's agent (Gen. 24); her pregnancy and bearing of Esau and Jacob (25:19–28); and her plotting with Jacob to deceive Isaac into giving Jacob the blessing he intended for Esau (chapter 27). The only story in which her level of participation is unclear is another instance of the wife-sister motif familiar from the Sarah cycle (26:6–11).

The story of Rebekah's engagement to Isaac is particularly intriguing, offering a glimpse of a social structure in which women appear to have considerable social recognition and responsibility for their own lives. Rebekah meets a stranger (Abraham's servant) and invites him to her parents' home for the night. Her family identification in the story is worth noting. The narrator introduces her as "Rebekah, who was born to Bethuel son of Milcah, the wife of Nahor, Abraham's brother" (24:15). Thus, she is identified first by her father's name (Bethuel), then by her grandmother's (Milcah), and third by her grandfather's (Nahor).[14] When asked her family, she answers similarly: "I am the daughter of Bethuel son of Milcah, whom she bore to Nahor" (24:24). Later, when Abraham's agent repeats the conversation, he remembers the order differently and quotes her as saying she is the "daughter of Bethuel, Nahor's son, whom Milcah bore to him" (24:47). Does this difference imply a tension between male- and female-oriented family relationships? This possibility is supported by another difference between Abraham's agent and the narrator. The agent asks, "Is there room in your *father's house* for us to spend the night?" but Rebekah runs to tell "her *mother's household*" what has happened (24:23, 28). In fact, we might wonder at first reading whether her father is still alive: it is her brother who plays the major role in welcoming the guests (24:29–32); gifts are given to Rebekah, her brother, and her mother (24:53); her brother and mother question the timing of her departure (24:55). Through all this, there is no indication that Rebekah's father is present. But at the end of the story it is Laban *and Bethuel* (Rebekah's father) who give permission for the marriage. He is present, then, although inactive in most of the story.

Rebekah has one more remarkable bit of autonomy in the story of her engagement. When Abraham's servant wants to return immediately, Rebekah's brother and mother would prefer that she have more time to prepare. They ask her whether she is ready to go, and it is by her decision that she departs when she does (24:55–61). This power of self-determination was also assumed by both Abraham and his agent. Before the trip, the agent asked what to do if the woman proved unwilling to accompany him (24:5), and Abraham agreed to release the agent from his oath in that case (24:8).

Rebekah is also the only matriarch to whom Yahweh gives special information about the future of her sons (25:22–23), information which may lead her later to conspire with Jacob against Isaac so that the younger son receives the blessing which his father intends for the elder (Gen. 27). She is thus one of the early trickster figures in Genesis, characters with limited legitimated power who use superior cleverness to thwart the intentions of figures with greater authority. Her son Jacob is a worthy successor in her tradition.

Leah and Rachel, two sisters, are wives (as well as first cousins) of Jacob. The story of their meeting and marriages (Gen. 29:9–30) sets up the principal dynamic tension of this cycle of stories: Rachel is Jacob's choice as wife, but Leah is forced on him by her father's trickery. Yahweh favors Leah with fertility because she is unloved (29:31). This sets up a rivalry in childbearing and lovemaking that includes maids as surrogate mothers and the use of mandrakes as fertility charms, with both wives and both maids bearing children (30:1–24). (Rachel also has one later child, Benjamin, and dies giving birth to him, 35:16–20.) The mandrakes incident includes the information that the women could decide which of them would have sex with their husband.

The cycle also includes the narrative of Rachel's role when the family leaves Laban's household (31:19–35). Without telling anyone, she steals her father's household gods and takes them with her. Laban pursues his departing relatives and scolds Jacob for taking his daughters without giving them a chance for a farewell—and for taking the gods. Knowing nothing about the gods, Jacob invites Laban to search for them and invokes the death penalty on anyone who might be found with them. Laban searches but does not find them, because Rachel has hidden them in the saddle of her camel and is sitting on them. She claims that the reason she does not get up to greet her father is that she is menstruating. (The narrator never tells whether her claim is true.) Jacob expresses righteous indignation at the apparently unjust accusation, and Laban goes home without the gods. If the narrator shares the later Israelite idea that bodily discharges are unclean, the joke may be more on the gods than on Laban. Not only are these supposed deities unable to protect themselves, but they are overpowered by the mere threat of menstrual blood.

Even this brief look at the matriarchs makes it clear that they are hardly paragons of virtue. In this, their narrative treatment parallels that of their husbands. Ancestors of Israel of both genders are revered for their role in creating a people, but there is no hesitance about admitting that they were also tricksters and liars.

Recurring Motifs

Several elements in the matriarch stories recur in tales of wives and mothers of other periods. Each of the matriarchs except Leah went through a time of *barrenness* before bearing children. This is also the case with the mothers of several other notable biblical figures, including the mother of Samson (unnamed in the text, Judg. 13:2–3), Hannah the mother of Samuel (1 Sam. 1:2), and Elizabeth the mother of John the Baptist (Luke 1:7).

This emphasis on barrenness indicates the importance of children within Israelite culture. In addition to their natural desire for offspring, Israelites found children an economic necessity. At an early age, children contributed to a family's productivity, and in adulthood they provided for the needs of elderly parents. In addition, children were the Israelite equivalent of immortality. Because the idea of an afterlife was outside Israelite thinking until the end of the Old Testament period, people strove to live on in their children.

The barrenness of the Israelite matriarchs has additional significance. The people looked back on these women as mothers of the whole people. The barrenness of the mothers, then, emphasizes the tenuousness of the descendants' own existence: their very being was a gift from Yahweh. In later stories (Hannah's or Elizabeth's barrenness, for example) there is a thematic recollection of the ancestral stories. The importance of these later women and their late-born sons is enhanced through the thematic resonances with the stories of the mothers of Israel.

Another recurring motif is the insistence on *marrying within the group*. Biblical texts show mixed attitudes about foreign women. On the one hand, they can be dangerous, whether they marry the hero (Samson's wives, Judg. 14-16; Solomon's wives, 1 Kings 11:3-4) or try to seduce men to whom they are not married (Potiphar's wife, Gen. 39). On the other hand, a foreign woman can also be a model of virtue and faithfulness (Ruth; unnamed Canaanite, Mark 7:24-30) and can figure in the royal (and, in the New Testament, messianic) genealogy (Rahab, Judg. 2, 6; Ruth; Matt. 1). The dialogue about whether to accept foreign women into Israel seems to reach a peak during the post-exilic period. Rejection of marriage to outsiders figures strongly in the reforms of Ezra and Nehemiah, while the book of Ruth may be a response to such exclusivism. As the tradition remembers him, Jesus shows himself in the tradition of Ruth rather than Ezra by displaying a remarkable degree of openness to non-Jewish women.

The *authority of mothers* is clearly presented in biblical texts. In the legal codes, Hebrew children are commanded to honor both parents; a son who is disobedient to father or mother is punished. The instruction of King Lemuel is presented as coming from his mother (Prov. 31:1-9), and other wisdom instructions in Proverbs urge obedience to mothers as well as fathers.[15] A specific case of maternal authority seems to be the queen mother (the mother of the reigning king). Contrast Bathsheba's submission as king's wife with her clear assumption of her rights as king's mother.[16]

Widows and Divorcees

Widows and divorcees are exceptions to the generalization that Israelites lived in male-headed households. Although they enjoyed a degree of autonomy not available to minor daughters or wives (for example, they could take vows that no man could annul, Num. 30:9), theirs was hardly an enviable position. Their households had no male heads, but the society's economic and legal systems assumed male-headed households. Thus, these unattached women were especially vulnerable members of society; as such, divorcées were awarded a monetary settlement, and widows received lifelong special legal protection. Biblical stories of widows reflect their marginal existence. Generally, their stories are included in the tradition only when they figure in a man's story. We can appreciate the predicament of Tamar (Gen. 38), the widow of Zarephath (1 Kings 17), Ruth, and the widow of Nain (Luke 7). How many more widows' and divorcées' stories went unrecorded we will never know.

Women's Religious Roles

Women's roles in the Israelite, early Jewish, and early Christian communities are difficult to reconstruct. At the outset, we must distinguish among popular religion, official religion, and canonical religion. There are significant differences among them. *Canonical religion* is religion as prescribed by the Bible in its final form. *Official religion* is the religion sponsored within a society. *Popular religion* is what the people actually believed and did.

Within ancient Israel, *canonical religion* presents the Jerusalem temple as the only legitimate sanctuary and its male priesthood as the cultic intermediaries. All women (and most men) were barred from the priesthood. The extent of women's participation in the Jerusalem cult is unclear except for those rituals specific to them (e.g., ritual purification after childbirth). Other religious ceremonies were household-based, however, and female participation can be expected. Women are presented as leaders during times when there was no temple in Jerusalem (before the building of Solomon's temple and between its destruction and the building of the second temple), and served as keepers of the meeting tent.

A major concern of canonical religion as a system is the maintenance of boundaries, including the significant boundary between ritually clean and unclean. In this system, bodily discharges are understood as unclean, including both women's menstrual flow and men's semen. Women were ritually unclean during the menstrual flow and for seven days following, after which time they cleansed themselves in a ritual bath. The participation of women in the cult during their entire lifetimes was curtailed because of the risk of "contamination" during their menstruating years.

The New Testament presents a rapidly changing picture of early church leadership in which women are acknowledged as leaders in the earliest texts and denied leadership roles in some of the later ones. Because of this variety, it is almost impossible to get a consistent picture of women's roles in canonical religion as presented in the New Testament.

Official religion varied significantly throughout the biblical period. During the periods before the monarchy, when social and political organization was family-centered, most religious practices were also family-based and probably involved both men and women. Women such as Miriam and Deborah are remembered as accepted leaders of the wilderness and pre-monarchic periods, apparently in religious as well as other spheres.

During the monarchic period, Jerusalem housed the central sanctuary of the southern realm. Other sanctuaries continued to function in both realms, however, including "high places" and the use of *'asheroth* (cultic pillars, possibly related to the goddess Asherah). Some believe that other deities were regularly worshiped along with Yahweh, and this is certainly true during some reigns (for example, Ahab and Jezebel in the northern realm). There were differences between the official religions of the two kingdoms, most notably the southern realm's emphasis on the Jerusalem temple and the Davidic dynasty. However, because our information is from texts edited later, neither southern nor northern official religion can be confidently reconstructed.

Popular religion is the most difficult to reconstruct. Archaeologists have discovered numerous figures of the female form, some of which appear to be pregnant. Some scholars speculate that these are images of a goddess or goddesses and that they may have been used in childbirth rituals, at sanctuaries, or both. Jeremiah objects to women's, men's, and children's involvement in preparing "cakes for the queen of heaven" (Jer. 7:18). Clearly, religious education was largely home-based and thus relied on the leadership of both women and men.

There may also have been specific women's rituals. One may be reflected in the sad story of Jephthah's unnamed daughter, sacrificed to Yahweh by her father in fulfillment of a foolish vow (Judg. 11:29–40). She requested and was granted two months reprieve, during which time she and her companions "bewailed her virginity on the mountains." The account concludes, "So there arose an Israelite custom that for four days every year the daughters of Israel would go out to lament the daughter of Jephthah the Gileadite."

Does this reflect a women's puberty ritual? It is possible but not clearly indicated in the text.

Religious Roles for Women

Prophets. There is no doubt at all that women were accepted as prophets, although it is not certain what the label means when applied to figures in the pre-monarchic period.

The story of Huldah, discussed earlier, is also presented in 2 Chronicles 34. In addition, Miriam (Exod. 15:20) and Deborah (Judg. 4:4), multifaceted leaders of early Israel, are labeled as prophets in the later tradition. Later prophetic women include Noadiah (Nehem. 6:14) and, in second-temple Judaism as presented in the New Testament, Anna (Luke 2:36). Unnamed women prophets are mentioned in Isaiah 8:3 and Acts 21:9. A prophecy about widespread prophesying by men and women occurs in Joel 2:28 (quoted in Acts 2:17). It is assumed in 1 Corinthians 11:5 that women prophesied in the early church. None of these texts expresses surprise that women are prophets. Even in the case of Noadiah, an opponent of Nehemiah whom he wants to discredit, her sex is not part of the explicit attack.

What is most striking about this list of prophets is that it includes women from all historical periods: Miriam from the wilderness era, Deborah from pre-monarchic Israel, Huldah and the unnamed woman in Isaiah from the monarchy, Noadiah from the time of resettlement, Anna from second-temple Judaism, and unnamed women in Acts and 1 Corinthians from early Christianity. Because it is unlikely that an increasingly male-dominated tradition would have written women's leadership into history, it is likely that women did exercise leadership throughout Israelite history and that they were recognized as prophets throughout the periods when prophecy existed.

Sage or Wise Woman. Several biblical characters are referred to as "wise women." Examples include women from Abel (2 Sam. 20) and Tekoa (2 Sam. 14). It is possible that "the fact that Joab approached the city walls to speak to [the wise woman of Abel] and that she could convince the town to deliver Sheba [indicates] that 'wise woman' was a title of some town official rather than a descriptive adjective."[17]

In later periods, sages (literally, "wise ones") were those responsible for instructing young people (usually, it is assumed, young men). Whether women could be sages in this sense is unclear. The possibility need not be dismissed, because "mother" appears alongside "father" to identify the giver of instruction in Proverbs (Prov. 1:8; 6:20; 10:1; 15:20; 23:25; 29:15). While other explanations for this usage exist, it is also possible that women could be sages in formal instructional settings.

Deacon, Congregational Matron, Missionary, Apostle. The personal greetings which close many of the New Testament epistles and the book of Acts indicate a variety of roles women held in the early church. Phoebe was a deacon (Rom. 16:1). Priscilla and her husband Aquila were prominent missionaries and teachers, leaders of a house church (Acts 18; Rom. 16:3-5; 1 Cor. 16:19; 2 Tim. 4:19). Nympha and Lydia host congregations (Col. 4:15; Acts 16:40). Junia is called a prominent apostle (Rom. 16:7).

Magician or Medium. Although canonical tradition rejected both magic and communication with the spirit world, there were practitioners of both arts in Israel.[18] Most of them were men, but a few women are included: the medium at Endor (1 Sam. 28) and female prophets who used magic (Ezek. 13).

Dancer, Musician, Singer. Women danced, made music, and sang at times of victory (Exod. 15:20-21; 1 Sam. 18:6) and at festivals (Judg. 21:21). They also sang laments (2 Sam. 1:24; Jer. 9:17). Wedding songs are another possibility. If the Song of Songs is associated with weddings, it may be noteworthy that the chorus is identified as "women of Jerusalem" (Song of Sol. 1:5, 2:7; 3:5; 5:8, 16; 8:4).

Author? Several interpreters have suggested female authorship in the biblical period, perhaps including authorship of texts now in the Bible. It is certainly plausible that the women who sang joyful or mournful songs may also have been the composers and lyricists responsible for producing them. It has even been suggested that women were creators of a number of biblical genres—not only victory song, lament, love poem, and wedding song, but also mirthful mockery, wisdom saying, and others.[19] Some argue for female authorship of the Song of Songs.[20] Harold Bloom even suggests that the author of the J source of the Pentateuch was a woman;[21] his argument is usually rejected but illustrates a trend toward openness about women's contributions to biblical materials that would have been nearly unthinkable a generation ago.

From our distance, it is impossible to prove that any specific text has a woman author, but it is equally impossible to prove that all biblical texts were written by men. Women may well be responsible for oral compositions that were later included in the written documents, and literary composition is not out of the question, especially for well-to-do urban women whose days were not consumed with basic survival tasks. Because Hebrew has a relatively simple alphabetic system, literacy was not necessarily limited to a closed social group in Israel.[22]

Women's Roles Outside Family and Religious Life

Most women in all periods did home-based work. By far, most of their time was spent on tasks directly related to survival. One estimate is that, in a typical household, an average Israelite woman may have spent four to five hours a day in field labor (planting, weeding, and harvesting) and up to two hours a day in grain processing (from milling to baking). In addition, during much of the year women would have spent several hours a day in textile production (preparing flax, carding and spinning thread, weaving cloth, and sewing garments). It is also possible that some everyday pottery and baskets were made locally by women. Childbearing and most early child care were also women's tasks. The sum of women's daily household activity was probably more than ten hours per day.[23]

Aside from these tasks, which belong to the extended family household, there were other roles for women, especially women not attached to such households either because they lived in cities or because they were widows or divorcées. Midwives were clearly a part of Israelite life in all periods. Prostitution was apparently also a normal part of Israelite life, although its frequency is masked in the biblical records. Fathers were apparently not forbidden to sell their daughters into prostitution until the time of deuteronomic legislation, late in the monarchy. There is no record that independent women (i.e., those whose sexuality was not under the authority of a male head of household) were forbidden to engage in prostitution. Indeed, this may have been the only means of support for some women unattached to male-headed households. The legitimacy of prostitution is illustrated by the story of two prostitutes who come to Solomon for judgment; he renders the judgment without questioning or objecting to their profession. Although many interpreters suppose that sacred prostitution existed in Israel, this is unclear; the meaning of the word that is sometimes translated as "sacred prostitute" is unclear.[24] No doubt the metaphoric use of adultery and prostitution for religious unfaithfulness contributed to the anti-prostitution attitude of late texts.

We know the least about the lives of slave women. Women were taken as war captives, and fathers could apparently sell their children into slavery. It is not always clear when servants were lifelong slaves and when they were indentured for a period. (Deuteronomic legislation did not allow lifelong enslavement of other Hebrews, but it is not clear that this law was ever enforced.) It is likely that, in large households, many of the everyday tasks were shared by free and slave women. It is also likely that free women assigned the most demeaning tasks to the slaves.

Women's Roles Idealized: Proverbs 31:10-31

Proverbs 31 contains a poem which begins, "A valiant woman who can find?"[25] Translators tend to render the expression "a capable wife"[26] or something similar, although when the word translated as "capable" is used of men it is normally translated as "strong" or "valiant."

This poem is as difficult to interpret as it is to label: many assume that it is a job description for a housewife. But if you read through the passage, you will note that this woman does more than any housewife—or even superwoman—can. Not only does she make the clothing for herself and her household (31:21-22), but she also buys the wool and flax (31:13), spins the thread (31:19), and even produces surplus garments to sell (31:24). Not only does she provide food for the household (31:15), but she also buys the fields and plants the vineyards (31:16). She rises while it is still night (31:15) and may remain up late into the night (31:18).[27] In addition to providing for the physical needs of her household in these ways, she also supports the needy (31:20), teaches wisdom (31:26), and may even engage in international trade (31:14).[28] She provides so well for her household that it appears her husband has nothing to do but sit at the city gate among the elders and compliment her.

If you are a woman who reads this as a literal job description, you must be despairing by now. No one could live up to such expectations. In fact, the text itself expresses recognition that this poem shows a woman doing better than the best: "Many women have done excellently, but you surpass them all" (31:29).

Who, then, is the woman in this passage? No flat equivalence does justice to the image, but the description leads us in two directions. On the one hand, it is an exaggerated account of the actual work of women in ancient Israel. On the other hand, the description is evocative of the images used earlier in Proverbs of wisdom, which is personified as a woman, "more precious than jewels" (31:10; see 3:15; 8:11); "a woman, fear of Yahweh" (31:30; see 1:7; 9:10; Job 28:28).[29] The passage may thus be both an idealization of women's productivity and a symbolic expression of the wisdom process and its rewards.[30]

What can we do with such a passage? I hope we don't burden women with the expectation that they can live up to its idealized terms. But we can celebrate it, both as a recognition of the value of women's work, within and beyond the household, and as a down-to-earth way of connecting personified wisdom with actual, human women's work.

Chapter Two

Women and Women

Dynamic Analogy

Women are powerful and important figures in biblical texts, yet the tradition has often skipped over them. In an interpretive tradition dominated by men and masculine concerns, women characters live in the margins. It is especially easy to sell the Bible short when it comes to women's relationships with other women. Yet women do relate to women—in sisterhood or in conflict, by choice or accidentally, in the context of men or when no men are on the scene. This chapter is an attempt to highlight a few of those relationships.

Although I have chosen these as women-and-women stories, I do not mean to suggest that there are no men in them or that the men are not important. However, because the male characters have received most of the attention in the interpretive tradition, one way to get a fresh perspective is to focus on the female characters and interpret the stories from their points of view.

In these stories, women relate to women, but they often do so in the context of relationships between women and men. This is understandable in a literary tradition in which men decided which texts were important enough to transmit. We might wonder how many women-and-women stories were shared in the places women gathered—at the town well or on the way home from funerals— stories that the keepers of the tradition never heard. Finally, though, we ought to rejoice that even a few women's stories survived.

Dynamic Analogy

Dynamic analogy is an interpretive method in which the reader identifies with characters in the text.[1] Using this method, you may find a character with whom it is easy to identify, one who is something like you. The richness of the method comes from identifying with various characters in the text rather than always the same one. Once you have found a character with whom it is fairly easy to identify, step outside yourself and try to imagine being one of the others. If possible, imagine the story from the point of view of each character in the text. Keep changing identifications until you have run out of possibilities for the stories.

Dynamic analogy is an open-ended method: there are no right answers. Most texts have gaps, places that leave the reader with unanswered questions. As you identify with various characters, you will find yourself filling in some of these gaps. This gap-filling is a kind of interpretive play. It is important to approach it with a sense of playfulness, an awareness that your interpretation is one possibility among many. When you fill gaps, you move from reading the text in front of you to writing a new text. This new text, too, can be rewritten—the gaps filled again in different ways. If you make a decision while you are identifying with one character, you may want to go back and change it when identifying with a different character.

Some of the most interesting gaps are in character development. In most texts, only two (or, at most, three) characters are developed, and the rest are merely sketched in to move the plot along. I think of these sketched-in characters as props in other characters' stories, and identifying with such props is likely to produce a new story rather than developing the story that is written in the text. Nonetheless, the differences between that new story and the existing text can give you a better sense of the choices an author has made, thus pointing you toward new interpretive directions for the existing text.

Dynamic analogy is a playful strategy in that it is always speculative. It can get you into the text and illuminate the text, but if you reach a point at which you are telling yourself that one way of identifying is so right that any other is wrong, you have lost the playfulness.

Although dynamic analogy is playful in that sense, it is not always easy or even enjoyable. Sometimes it is very difficult to find a way into a story: all of the characters may seem incomprehensible. At other times, you may find yourself identifying most clearly with a character you do not like or respect and find it painful to enter the story in such a role. I have found that when I stick it out and make the difficult or painful identifications, I learn the most about both the text and myself.

Hagar and Sarah

Read: Genesis 16 and 21

The Story. Sarah is Abraham's wife. Hagar, Sarah's maid, is an Egyptian. Although Abraham has been promised descendants, he and Sarah have no children. Sarah suggests that Hagar serve as surrogate mother.

Abraham and Hagar conceive a child. When Hagar realizes that she is pregnant, she looks "with contempt" on Sarah. Sarah then treats Hagar harshly, and Hagar runs away into the desert. While there, she sees the angel of Yahweh, who sends her back. She bears a son whom Abraham names Ishmael.

Some time later, Sarah and Abraham have a son of their own whom Abraham names Isaac. After Isaac is weaned, Sarah, seeing Ishmael playing, tells Abraham to throw Hagar and Ishmael out of the household. Abraham is distressed and prays about the matter. God tells him to do as Sarah says, but promises to "make a nation" of Ishmael as well. Abraham supplies Hagar with food and water, and she leaves with the child.

When the water is gone, Hagar expects that she and the child will die. The angel of God hears her or the boy crying and promises Hagar, "I will make a great nation of him." Then "God opened her eyes and she saw a well of water. She went, and filled the skin with water, and gave the boy a drink."

Genesis says nothing about the rest of Hagar's life.

Analysis. The story of Hagar and Sarah is the first biblical narrative of conflict between women. It is a class conflict, between rich woman and domestic servant, owner and slave. It is also a conflict of peoples: Sarah is Hebrew and Hagar is Egyptian. Later Israelites would be ambivalent about Egypt and Egyptians, which they see both as a part of their heritage and as the source of their enslavement. Here, however, it is the Egyptian who is the slave and the Hebrew who is the unjust taskmistress.

Sarah and Abraham are both characters whose names are changed by divine command. In chapter 16, they appear as Sarai and Abram, but by chapter 21 they have been given the names by which the tradition knows them. I have chosen to use their traditional names, Sarah and Abraham, throughout.

The background of the story is God's promise to Abraham that he will father a great nation. At first the mother of the great nation is unspecified, so Sarah's plan to have Hagar bear the child is plausible as an attempt to bring the promise to fulfillment. Between the two chapters of the Sarah-Hagar conflict, the promise becomes more specific: Sarah is to bear the child of the promise. At this assurance, first Abraham and then Sarah laugh.

This background of promise makes the final scene more striking: the angel of God promises Hagar that her child will be the ancestor of a great nation. This is the only time that the "promise to the ancestors" is given to a woman rather than to a man.

The biblical text presents a complicated story in two acts. In the first, Hagar chooses to run away; in the second, Sarah has Abraham drive Hagar away. Many interpreters believe that, instead of two separate stories, chapters 16 and 21 reflect two different versions of the same tradition. Yet in the book of Genesis, the two are in counterpoint to each other.

The second story especially is difficult in context. The intervening chapters suggest that a number of years have passed; the implied chronology would make Ishmael at least thirteen years old at the time of chapter 21. Yet the action in the story suggests a very young child: his mother carries him. The story also acknowledges that between the Hebrews and those they considered Ishmaelites, there are both kinship and estrangement.

Although these chapters tell Hagar and Sarah's story, they do so from a male perspective. Perhaps it is not surprising that the tradition chooses to present women in conflict. The concerns of patriarchy in a male-oriented society turn women against each other and urge members of groups labeled "other" to use their limited power against each other instead of against the system which uses both of them. But, the tyranny of the system must not be used to excuse Sarah (and those of us who identify with Sarah) in the oppression of those who have less power and fewer options.

This is also an Israelite story. The people telling it know from the first that Isaac will be born to Sarah, that Sarah and not Hagar is their mother. For its Israelite audience, the dramatic tension in the story does not derive from the question, "Which mother and child will prevail?" but rather, "How will my ancestors, Sarah and Isaac, overcome the threat represented by Hagar and Ishmael?"

Dynamic Analogy. Try applying dynamic analogy to this text. Imagine being a young woman, a foreigner, living as a domestic servant in the home of a childless couple. But "domestic servant" does not really describe your situation. You are a slave in a foreign land, and your only support comes from the wealthy couple who own you. What if you were asked—forced—to serve as surrogate mother for a child that would legally be the offspring of the couple? Would you agree willingly, knowing that bearing a child to your owner might improve your living conditions? Would you perceive it as legalized rape? Would you become angry at the man who forced himself upon you, the woman who had the idea to offer your body to atone for her barrenness?

When you became pregnant, would you feel shamed or vindicated? Might you develop a sense of superiority over the older, rich woman? What if she became jealous of you and your blossoming pregnancy? What if she made your life even more difficult, not only increasing your work but abusing you verbally and perhaps physically? Perhaps you would decide to run away—even if the only place to run were the desert.

In the desert, you are ready to die—hungry and thirsty, with no hope of help from any source. Then you have a mystical experience—see a presence and hear a voice. The voice tells you to return to your mistress. You are certain that this is the voice of God, so—although you do not want to—you return. You remain with the couple throughout the remainder of your pregnancy, then give birth to a son whom your mistress takes as her own.

Now try switching identifications. Suppose that you are the wife, that you desperately want to become pregnant and have tried until it is no longer physically possible. What if, in addition to your and your husband's desire for a child and a future for your family, there is a sense of destiny, of divine promise? You might turn to this girl (yes, you think of her as a girl even though she is woman enough to carry a child) to fulfill your and your husband's dreams. Once she is pregnant, she appears to you to be swelling in pride even before her body begins to expand. It is clear to you that she is proud of her connection with your husband and scornful of you, who are unable to conceive. Yet you must watch her every day. You are jealous, not only of the life growing in her but even of the morning sickness and backache and swelling ankles. Perhaps you note the foods that distress her and insist on being served just those foods for breakfast. You casually command her to lift and carry more than before. You wanted this pregnancy and arranged for it to happen, but now that it has you are in pain. You believe that you have been wronged. You strike out at her in senseless, useless anger, trying to wound her ego. You are angry, not only at her but also at your husband. You may know that it doesn't make sense, but that hardly matters. You hurt, and she reminds you day by day and hour by hour of your pain. She must suffer.

She does suffer, of course. Wounded in pride, perhaps also in body, she slinks around the household. You enjoy her humiliation, even increase it. Then one day she disappears. You are stunned. She has nowhere to go. She will return, you are sure. And yes, she does return and soon gives birth to a healthy boy. Now the household includes the married couple, the surrogate mother, and her growing child.

Then the impossible happens. You become pregnant. You are too old to conceive, but you are with child. You carry it to term and give birth to a son.

Yes, you are a mother now—not just an adoptive mother, but a physical mother of a baby boy. You rejoice and yet, as time goes on, you become more and more disturbed watching the two children, your infant boy and the slave woman's older son. Oh, what a foolish plan it had been! Why had you concocted that crazy scheme, the idea of the surrogate having a baby with your husband? It was stupid. You should have known that you would become pregnant, that it was a matter of divine promise. Now you can see that you have made a foolish mistake, but it is too late.

One day you notice, as you have countless times before, the slave woman's boy, the firstborn of the household, outside playing.[2] You are filled with rage that you do not understand. Here is the boy playing as though he owned the place—but he should not. Your son is the child of promise, the one who ought to inherit all that had been his father's. The slave's boy might be the firstborn, but yours is the miracle child. You want the usurper removed. You go to your husband and insist that he throw out the boy and his insolent mother.

It is not easy. Your husband resists and insists on praying about it. This frightens you because you are not sure that your rage is godly. Finally, your husband agrees. God has affirmed your plan. The boy and his mother are to be removed.

What then? Are you relieved? Do you get on with your life and forget about them? Or do you lie awake at night wondering, going over the past, wishing there had been another way? Are you closer to your husband, or does the image of the absent women stand like a wall between you? What of your relationship with your son? Does he understand himself to be the cause of the absence of the others? Does he mind?

Now become the surrogate again. You know that the wife resents you, dislikes you. Even though her womanhood has been vindicated through childbearing, she remains cold and abusive toward you, the mother of her husband's firstborn. She grows cold, too, toward your son—her son legally, but both of you know that he is yours. You are proud of that—proud of the physical signs of your maternity, proud of his African features.

One day when your son is playing outside, the wife sees him and becomes enraged. She goes to her husband and demands that you and the boy be thrown out. He is uncertain. You know he doesn't want to do it. You trust his feelings for the child if not for you. He retreats, considers, prays. You are amazed when you learn that he has agreed to his wife's scheme. He packs up a few days' supplies and sends you out.

Wandering in the desert, you and the boy are hungry and thirsty. There is no help anywhere. You realize that the two of you will die. Resigned, you lay the child under a bush so that at least he will not die of sunstroke—he will be as comfortable as possible while he starves to death. Then you crawl off to wait for your own death. You are aware of the sound of wailing. Is it your own voice or the child's?

Again comes the vision (hallucination? How can you be sure?) You sense a presence, a voice. The voice speaks a promise: your son will live, and he will become the ancestor of a great nation. Then the presence shows you a well. In the middle of the desert, there is water to sustain your life and that of your son. Perhaps you tremble as you approach, thinking it a dream, expecting the well to dissolve before your eyes. But it is real, substantial. You drink. You give water to your son. You and he will live.

What happens to you as you become Hagar, then Sarah, then Hagar again? How do you perceive the other woman? Is she a person to you or a role?

For me, it is both difficult and painful to enter into the story of Hagar and Sarah. I know that by social class, marital status, and race, I am our culture's equivalent of Sarah. I resist the recognition that my privilege and selfishness dispossess Hagar. I want to rage against the system that pits woman against woman, that makes my status depend on her degradation. And yet I must admit: when poor women and their children become homeless, it supports my privilege. And I do not stop it. Yes, the system is at fault, but so am I.

While it is painful for me to identify with Sarah, it is difficult in a different way for me to identify with Hagar, the woman with no-where to turn. When the angel of Yahweh comes to her the first time, Hagar is sent back to Sarah, her abuser. It is scandalous that a biblical story can be used by those in our own time who, claiming God's authority, send women back to settings in which they have been abused. The second time Hagar is in the desert, returning is not an option; she has been cast out of the household of Sarah and Abraham. What can the angel tell her this time? This time it is a blessing: her son will live and father a great nation. The blessing is a great relief, yet it is sad. Made homeless by the rich and powerful Hebrew couple who are responsible for her, she is rescued by a God she must also perceive as powerful and Hebraic—and male.[3] Does Hagar long for the gods and goddesses of Egypt? To whom would she look for rescue if she were not on Hebrew territory?

The final sadness is that the story ends not with reconciliation between Hagar and Sarah, Ishmael and Isaac, but with two separate (and sometimes warring) nations identified in the tradition as children of Abraham.

Shiprah, Puah, Moses' Mother, Moses' Sister, Pharaoh's Daughter, Attendants

Read: Exodus 1:15-2:10
The Story. The king of Egypt (the pharaoh) orders Shiprah and Puah, Hebrew midwives, to kill all newborn Hebrew boys. They do not carry out the order, claiming that the Hebrew women have short

labor and give birth before the midwives arrive. God blesses
Shiprah and Puah. The pharaoh extends the command to kill
Hebrew boys to everyone. Throw Hebrew boys into the Nile, he
orders.

After hiding her newborn son for three months, one Hebrew
mother puts him into a papyrus basket, which she places in the
river, near the banks. The baby's sister watches from a distance and
sees the pharaoh's daughter come to bathe in the river. When the
princess finds the child, the sister appears and offers to find a
wetnurse for him; she leads the pharaoh's daughter to the boy's
birth mother. The princess then pays the boy's mother to nurse the
child. After the baby is weaned, the mother returns him to the
pharaoh's daughter, who names him Moses.

Analysis. The story is set a number of generations after the period
of the ancestors but before the Hebrews have settled in their land
and become a nation. They are living in Egypt, where for a time
they were honored guests. Now they have become forced laborers.
The Egyptian king (or pharaoh) is afraid of their potential power,
and in an attempt to weaken them, he has increased their
workload. The command to kill boy Hebrews fits into the fear that
the Israelites will become strong enough to pose a threat to the
Egyptians.

From the perspective of the book of Exodus and the Bible as a
whole, much good comes from the events narrated in this story.
Not only is the life of the child preserved, but through him God
effects the deliverance of Israel. The story is a preamble to the
Exodus, letting us know that Moses is a Hebrew but also has
strong connections with the Egyptian royal court.

Yahweh is not an explicit character in the story, and nothing
contrary to nature happens, yet both Jewish and Christian traditions have seen the power of God active in preserving the life of the
future liberator. Elsewhere in the Bible, Moses' mother is identified
as Jochabed and his sister as Miriam, but in this story both are
unnamed.

The text has resonances with other narratives. Its ancient
audiences may well have noticed parallels with the Akkadian legend
of the birth of Sargon the Great. That ruler's mother also set him
afloat in the reeds in a pitch-lined basket.[4] For readers of the
Hebrew Bible, the story resonates with other texts in which water is

a threat to survival or a means of deliverance, including the story of the great flood, the crossing of the Red (or Reed) Sea during the Exodus from Egypt, and the crossing of the Jordan River to enter the land which would become Israel.

The prominence of women in the text is striking. They are bold and effective while playing out traditional female roles—child care, pity for a foundling, playing trickster in the absence of socially legitimated power, even lazing in the bath.

Traditional male power has little effect. Aside from the pharaoh's command which precipitates the whole chain of events (yet is ineffective, as the one Hebrew who will threaten him lives), all of the action is carried out by women. Particularly surprising is the absence of Moses' father. Surely men wanted sons in that age, as in most times. Yet the storytellers leave him sleeping in the margins of the text while women determine the fate of his son. Although another strand of tradition identifies Aaron as Moses' older brother, for the purposes of this story Aaron does not exist.

All of the Hebrew women engage in trickster behavior: from a powerless position, each connives to thwart the pharaoh's command. Shiprah and Puah seek to persuade the pharaoh that they are unable to obey his command. (Apparently they succeed; we would expect him to punish them otherwise.) The baby's mother obeys the letter but not the intent of the law by putting her child into the river but first providing the protection of the waterproofed basket. The sister preserves the family by tricking the pharaoh's daughter into hiring the boy's mother as wetnurse.

The text does not tell us what the characters know or how carefully they plan. Do the child's mother and sister expect the princess to find the baby? Do they count on her womanly sympathy to counteract her royal father's decree? Does she defy her father's command deliberately, or might she be unaware of it?

Dynamic Analogy. What happens when you are one of the midwives? Tell the story from Shiprah or Puah's point of view, defiantly lying to the pharaoh about your disobedience. Are you present anywhere later in the story? Are you aware of the boy's survival? If so, how does it make you feel? Does it affect your own behavior?

Now imagine being the child's mother. Can you imagine feeling the love that would move you first to hide your baby and then to make him a tiny ark and set him afloat in the Nile where the princess might find him? Can you imagine wanting an Egyptian, especially a member of the royal household, to raise him—when it is the Egyptian king who seeks his death? Do you fear that the pharaoh will see him and order him killed after all? Or do you trust that even the pharaoh feels parental love and will not order the death of his daughter's foster child?

Can you be the older sister, taking care of the baby and even keeping him in the family? As the sister, do you act out of love for the baby, love for your and the baby's mother, a sense of duty, a longing for recognition ("everyone is making a big fuss about the boy—let's see how I can get some attention"), or childish adventure? The sister's motivation is left open in the text, as is her age. She is the story's boldest trickster, and her role is invested with rich irony: "I'll find someone to nurse him; think of all the Hebrew women whose breasts are aching, full of milk for killed babies." She takes him home: "Look, mama, a baby. Can we raise him?"

Can you identify with the princess, finding a baby in the water? There is very little information about her in the text, so you must decide how to fill the gaps. Is she a child or a young woman? Does she consider the baby a plaything, a sort of living doll? Has she been kept ignorant of her father's decree, or does she disobey it deliberately? Might she be a subversive figure, outraged at her father's decree and seeing in the child an opportunity to undo it? Does she sense a fine irony in her tyrannic father paying to feed, clothe, and educate one of the hated Hebrews?

What of the daughter's attendants? Here, too, you must fill in gaps. Are they slave or free? Do they identify with the Hebrews or scorn them? Do they gladly join the plan to adopt the baby and find it a wetnurse, or do they fear the royal father's anger? The specific elements of their reaction will vary depending on how you fill in the gaps about their and the princess' knowledge. If she is unaware of the decree and they are not, do they contemplate telling her about it? Do they in fact tell her? If all know of the decree, do they speak of it? Do they encourage her to find a Hebrew woman to nurse the baby? Do they suspect that the woman is the child's mother?

We might imagine other women around the margins of the story, Hebrews whose sons were not saved. How do they respond to a woman in their midst who is paid by the pharaoh's daughter to nurse her own child, when their children have been sacrificed to the Nile?

The story's emphasis on women characters may provide a special challenge for men attempting dynamic analogy. In our culture, stories about women tend to be stories for women only. Traditional male interpretation has read this story as "the birth of Moses," and focused on God's thwarting of the pharaoh. It will take some courage and imagination for men to play the women's roles in the text, but the rewards will make the effort worthwhile.

Deborah, Jael, Sisera's Mother, Wise Ladies, Lyricists and Singers

Read: Judges 4-5

The Story. In pre-monarchic Israel, while the Israelites are under the rule of Jabin, a Canaanite ruler, Deborah is a prophet, judge, and military leader. She tells Barak that Yahweh commands him to go into battle against Jabin's army, which is headed by Sisera. Yahweh promises Barak victory. Barak agrees to go, but only if Deborah accompanies him. She agrees, but she warns him not to expect glory for himself: "for Yahweh will sell Sisera into the hand of a woman."

Barak and Deborah set out. Barak's army completely wipes out Sisera's army, and only Sisera is left. He runs to the tent of Jael, the wife of a Kenite who is allied with the Canaanites. Jael invites him into her tent and covers him with a rug. He asks for a drink of water, and she gives him milk. Then, while he is sleeping, she takes a tent peg and hammers it through his head. Barak comes seeking Sisera. Jael shows him the corpse. The Israelites go on to destroy Jabin. Deborah and Barak sing a song celebrating the victory as Yahweh's.

Analysis. Deborah is the only woman judge in Israel. ("Judge" is a general term that covers a variety of leadership roles.) In Deborah's case, leadership apparently involved rendering legal decisions, transmitting the word of Yahweh to the people, and leading a military expedition. Deborah's story is told twice in Judges, first in a prose narrative (chapter 4), and then in a victory song (chapter 5). Although the general outline of events is the same in both accounts, details and emphasis differ. This interpretation emphasizes the poetic version in Judges 5.

Although the song acclaims Deborah as "a mother in Israel" and Barak as one who leads captives away, it is primarily a celebration of Yahweh as victor. It notes which tribes joined in the battle and which did not (although the details in 5:14-18 do not quite match the description in 4:10). The battle takes on cosmic proportions when even the stars fight against Sisera (5:20) and the wadi Kishon sweeps them away (5:21).

Jael is acclaimed as "most blessed of women." Her killing of Sisera is described in detail, as is his death: "He sank, he fell,/ he lay still at her feet;/ at her feet he sank, he fell;/ where he sank, there he fell dead." Interpreters have noted the language of sexual conquest in this description.[5]

The song adds a scene describing Sisera's mother waiting for his return, wondering what has kept him so long, and presents an imaginary conversation between her and her wise ladies. "Are they not finding and dividing the spoil?—A girl or two for every man; spoil of dyed stuffs . . . embroidered for my neck as spoil?" It concludes, "So perish all your enemies, O Yahweh!/ But may your friends be like the sun as it rises in its might." As a postscript, the text adds: "And the land had rest forty years."

The victory song is a complicated text. Because we read it as a text, we know all of the women in it as literary characters, not as living human beings. But some of the characters are more hypothetical than others, fictional even from the point of view of the narration itself.

The most real of the women characters are Deborah and Jael, who are presented as real, historical figures. The text presents other women in the imagination of the lyricists: Sisera's mother and her "wise ladies," who may or may not have existence outside the text. They in turn imagine captive Israelite women, whom we know not to exist. In addition to these literary characters, we may guess that other women stand behind the text. Although the song is introduced as being sung by Deborah and Barak, its third-person praise of them suggests that they are not its authors. If indeed the victory song is a women's genre in ancient Israel, the lyricists may have been unnamed Israelite women.

There are only two sets of direct relationships among the women—Jael with Deborah as spy to commander and Sisera's mother with her wise ladies. The first of these is apparently straightforward and cooperative: Deborah and Jael are both working for the same side and toward the same end.

Sisera's mother and her "wisest of ladies" appear in a conversation imagined by the lyricists. They are imagining the spoils being divided by Sisera and the other Canaanites, whom these women presume to be victors (although we readers know otherwise). They too appear to speak in harmony; reading the text, we are not even sure whether the quoted words belong to the mother or the wise ladies. Yet we might wonder how real this apparent cooperation is. Who are these "wise ladies" and what is their relationship to Sisera's mother? Are they Canaanite noblewomen, whom we might suppose to speak in harmony with Sisera's mother? Or are they servants or slaves? If so, how did they come into a state of servitude? Might they be spoils from a previous war?

The text does not tell us. And because they are not real people but characters imagined by the lyricist, there is no reality to the question, "Are they servants or are they nobles?" The text leaves it open. We are free to imagine them either way.

These women in turn imagine other women, Israelites, whom they suppose to be spoils of war for the Canaanites. This fact may be difficult to acknowledge—women fantasizing the kidnaping and rape of other women. It is even more bizarre if Israelite women composed this song and were imagining Sisera's mother indulging in this cruel fantasy. Israelite women authors here might be enjoying the fantasy of Canaanite women fantasizing the rape of Israelite women (who might include the authors and composers of this song).

The song involves an inversion of sexual imagery. First, we do not normally think of women fantasizing the rape of other women. Beyond that, Deborah's role as commander is a socially masculine one. The presentation of Jael mixes images of traditionally feminine behavior (shelter, blanket, milk) with traditionally masculine aggression. The song dwells on Sisera's death in terms that are not appropriate if you assume, with the prose narrative, that he is lying down when she kills him. But the language is that of sexual aggression: a conquest, he lies between her legs. Even the cruel fantasy in which the Israelite lyricists imagine the Canaanites fantasizing the rape of Israelites is foreshadowed in verse 7: "The peasantry prospered in Israel,/ they grew fat on plunder." The line may sound relatively innocent on first reading—until verse 30, where we discover a girl [literally, "womb"] or two for every man" to be part of that plunder.[6]

Dynamic Analogy. Imagine that you are a woman in time of war. No doubt you will relate most closely to your own people, male or female. Less directly, you may also relate to those who are caught up in the same war on the other side.

You might be the woman general, planning your strategy, deploying your troops. (Of course, if you are Deborah, the strategy is not your own: Yahweh is directing you.) Are you the only woman directly involved in the fighting? Do you know Jael? Does a side of you worry about trusting a Kenite, a supposed ally of the Canaanites? How do you think of the Canaanite women? Do you perceive them as real people, or is their potential death or rape merely collateral damage—regrettable but normal in war.

What if you are Jael? You are married to a Kenite and are thus formally allied with the Canaanites. Yet you are willing to kill a Canaanite for the sake of Israelite victory. Why? Does the sexual imagery of the murder scene belong to the way you relate the story, or is it an embellishment on the part of the lyricists? If it is yours, what makes you want to "rape" Sisera?

What if you are Sisera's mother? Do you so dehumanize the Israelite women as to rejoice in their being spoil for the soldiers, no more significant than the "dyed stuffs embroidered" that will grace your neck? Or do you rush from the mention of "a girl or two" to the embroidered and dyed work because you cannot bear to dwell on the captivity of the "girls"?

What if you are among the wise ladies? Do you answer Sisera's mother or not? Do you identify with the captives or are you hoping that your own sons will also get some of that spoil?

Finally, what if you are among the Israelite women who may have composed this song? What is in your mind as you dwell on the death of Sisera and fantasize the soon-to-be-debunked fantasies of the Canaanite women? Is it easier to deal with the idea of them as "spoils of war" if you assume that they have been wishing the same for you? Or is this one more example of the dehumanizing effect of war, of a human need to perceive the enemy as subhuman?

Some of these roles will no doubt be more difficult to take on than others. Of course, you need not admire characters in order to try to experience the story from their point of view. You may want to try writing a new story or song that would incorporate the various points of view. How would you feel as a woman general or spy? How would you deal with war as a woman whose son or husband is fighting? Do you think about the women on the other side? If so, how do you imagine them? When the war is over, will you sing? Will your song celebrate victory or mourn death and loss?

How should women's voices be raised in time of war?

Naomi, Ruth, Orpah, Bethlehemite Women

Read: Ruth 1:1–22; 4:13–22 (or the entire book of Ruth)
The Story. The setting is pre-monarchic Israel and neighboring Moab, about the same time as the story of Deborah. A family (Elimelech and Naomi and their two sons, Mahlon and Chilion) migrates from Bethlehem in Judah to Moab. There the father dies. The sons marry, and then they also die, before either of them fathers a child with his Moabite wife.

Finally, the news comes that the famine in Judah is over. The mother, Naomi, decides to return home. The two daughters-in-law say that they will return with her. "Turn back," Naomi says, "each of you to her mother's house." One of the younger women, Orpah, acquiesces to her mother-in-law's request. The other, Ruth, refuses:

> Do not press me to leave you
>   or to turn back from following you!
> Where you go, I will go;
>   where you lodge, I will lodge;
> your people shall be my people,
>   and your God, my God.
> Where you die, I will die—
>   there I will be buried.

When Naomi and Ruth arrive in Bethlehem, they are greeted by the local women. It is a homecoming for Naomi, and representatives of the welcome wagon come out to greet her. But she refuses to play the part, rejecting their embraces, denying their joy:

> Stop calling me Honey;
>   instead, call me Bitter,
>   for Shaddai has dealt bitterly with me.

> I went away full,
>> but Yahweh has brought me back empty.
>
> Why call me Honey
>> when Yahweh has been harsh to me
>> and Shaddai has brought disaster on me?[7]

In the final scene of the story, Ruth has met and married Boaz, a well-to-do relative of Elimelech. The Bethlehem women rejoice with Naomi at the birth of a son to Ruth and Boaz: "For your daughter-in-law who loves you, who is more to you than seven sons, has borne him." When Naomi becomes the child's nurse, the women exclaim, "A son has been born to Naomi!" They name him Obed, and he becomes the grandfather of King David.

Analysis. If the story is familiar to us, and especially if we are reading from within the Jewish or Christian tradition, we may not recognize how strange it is, even from an Israelite perspective. First, it begins with "a certain man of Bethlehem" who had a wife and two sons. Based on this beginning, a reader might expect the story to focus on the man and his sons. By the fifth verse, however, all the men are dead, and two additional women have come on stage. A typical (that is, male-oriented) story seems to be turning into a women's story.

Second, at this point in the text, Ruth does not fit into cultural expectations. Naomi's decision to return to her homeland is not surprising, as there is nothing to keep her in Moab. And, Orpah also appears to behave normally by following the expressed wishes of her mother-in-law. By returning to her mother's house, she remains within her own culture.

Ruth, however, is different. She expresses her faithfulness to her mother-in-law by disobeying her. She seems to find it easier to leave her family and her native land than to leave her mother-in-law. Her promise sounds less like something a woman would say to her mother-in-law than like something she would say to her husband. In fact, the passage has been borrowed for use in marriage services. Although we may rejoice at reclaiming the text as a declaration of woman-to-woman faithfulness, it is not by accident that we have found this pledge of steadfastness until death relevant for weddings. This is how we think of marriage; it is not how we usually think of in-laws.

As we continue to read the story, the beginning seems increasingly odd. Since Orpah disappears after verse 14, what is she doing in the text at all? It would have been a tidier story if the narrator had concentrated on one son and his marriage. The presence of two sons serves partly to show how much Naomi had lost: she had excess but lost everything. The greater effect, however, is to emphasize the different choices Orpah and Ruth make. Having set up the contrast, however, the author does not explain these differences. Because Orpah does not figure in the rest of the story, her function here is to point up Ruth's faithfulness as a choice that she did not have to make.

Most of the book tells of the meeting and courtship of Ruth and Boaz in which Ruth, at Naomi's instigation, takes the initiative. Boaz is a relative of Elimelech, and Ruth calls on him to enter into a levirate marriage with her.[8] After persuading a nearer relative to relinquish his claim, Boaz and Ruth marry.

What is most remarkable about the story from an Israelite perspective is that a Moabite woman is both presented positively and given a place in the genealogy of the great king David. Some interpreters suppose that this story was told during the post-exilic period, when anti-Moabite prejudices ran strong.

Dynamic Analogy. Try identifying with Naomi. Her life appears to begin normally enough; she is married and has two sons. Then things begin to go awry when famine comes to Judah and the family must travel from Bethlehem (which ironically means literally "house of bread") to Moab to find bread. While there, the two sons marry Moabite women. We might wonder how Naomi accepts their decision; marriage within the group is a long-standing Israelite tradition. In Moab, life for Naomi takes a decided turn for the worse when first her husband and then her sons die. As Naomi, how do you handle this change from married mother to childless widow in a foreign land? Are you angry at your daughters-in-law? Are you angry at God? When word arrives that the Judahite famine is over, you decide to return home, and you urge your daughters-in-law to return to their mothers' houses. It is a strange homecoming that you plan. In exile, you have lost what little you once had. You are returning empty—with no family, possessions, or expectations. Do you secretly hope that the two younger women will deny your request and accompany you, or it is better to come back alone than with the foreign widow of a dead son? Are you ashamed of Ruth and Orpah and their Moabite accents and gods?

Now become Orpah. Is Naomi's insistence that you stay behind a source of relief, or sadness, or both? Are you happy to return to your mother's house, or will life as the widow of a foreigner be difficult for you? Will you miss Ruth? Are there prospects for another marriage? Will you spend the rest of your life in the family household? Will you have to support yourself? If so, do you have any options—except perhaps prostitution?

And what if you are Ruth? Why do you go along to Bethlehem? Why do you force yourself on a mother-in-law who does not seem to want you? What is there for you in Judah? What would your life be like if you remained in Moab?

Play with these possibilities. At the juncture where Orpah leaves and Ruth stays, which are you? Do you find yourself easily closing one chapter of your life and moving on to the next, or do you work at preserving relationships?

When Naomi and Ruth arrive in Bethlehem and are greeted by the townswomen, Naomi cries out in bitterness. How do you identify with the Bethlehem women? Are you stunned? Do you wonder why Naomi refuses to play her proper part? Trying to be friendly, are you put off? In your heart, do you think, *This is what you get for going to Moab; I'll bet God killed your men for leaving holy territory*, or do you reach out to find the lost friend behind the bitterness?

As Naomi, are you surprised to hear yourself uttering these bitter words? Is this the speech you rehearsed on the trek from Moab, or does the encounter with the Bethlehem women bring out a pain you did not know you felt?

If you are Ruth, do you feel awkward? Do you feel the local women judging you? How conscious are you of your foreign accent? Do you gain a better understanding of how Naomi must have felt in Moab? How hard do you try to fit in?

At the end of the story, when everyone is happy, dynamic analogy may become easier. As Naomi, you have regained your standing in the community. How do you feel as you hold the child that came from Ruth's body? Is it any substitute for your own lost sons? Do the townswomen's words ring true when they say that

Ruth is "more to you than seven sons"?

As the Bethlehem women, are you secretly holding your breath, hoping that Naomi will not turn bitter again? Are your glad songs a recognition of her joy or a plea that she accept what joy God has given her? Do you understand Ruth finally to be one of your own?

As Ruth, are you happy? Is it all right for your child to become Naomi's, for your joy to belong to this community? Do you still think of Moab and the family you left behind, or are you secure in your new home, honored by adopted compatriots?

Whichever place you have chosen, do you have a sense of God's providence in your story?

Elizabeth and Mary of Nazareth

Read: Luke 1:5–56
The Story. Elizabeth and Zechariah are elderly and childless. Zechariah is a priest. In the temple, Zechariah has a vision in which an angel announces to him that his wife will bear a son. Zechariah asks how this can happen, since both he and his wife are old. The angel punishes Zechariah's lack of faith: "Because you did not believe my words . . . you will become mute, unable to speak, until the day these things occur." Zechariah comes out of the temple unable to speak, and people realize that he has had a vision. Elizabeth does conceive a child. She understands this as divine favor and the removal of the disgrace of barrenness.

When Elizabeth is in her sixth month of pregnancy, God sends the same angel, Gabriel, to Mary in Nazareth. He greets her with "Greetings, favored one! The Lord is with you." Mary is perplexed and wonders about the greeting. The angel tells her not to be afraid and announces that she will bear a son, who "will be great, and will be called the Son of the Most High, and the Lord God will give to him the throne of his ancestor David. He will reign over the house of Jacob forever, and of his kingdom there will be no end." Mary asks, "How can this be, since I am a virgin?" The angel says the Holy Spirit will be involved, and tells Mary that Elizabeth, a relative, is now in her sixth month of pregnancy. Mary says, "Here am I, the servant of the Lord; let it be with me according to your word." The angel leaves.

Mary hurries to Elizabeth's home and greets her. Elizabeth's unborn child leaps in her womb; filled with the Spirit, Elizabeth says, "Blessed are you among women, and blessed is the fruit of your womb," and calls Mary "the mother of my Lord." Mary sings a song rejoicing that God reverses the fortunes of both the lowly and the mighty. After visiting for three months, Mary returns home.

Analysis. There are strong parallels between the stories of Elizabeth and Mary:[9]

1. Conception unexpected due to age of mother
2. Appearance of angel Gabriel
3. Parent "troubled"
4. Angel telling parent not to fear
5. Angel promising a son
6. Angel giving name for unborn son
7. Son will be "great"
8. Parent asks how
9. Parent given sign
10. Joy at birth of son
11. God's activity sensed after circumcision
12. Canticle sung after circumcision
13. Both sons "grew and became strong"

The parallels also include contrasts. Elizabeth was considered too old to bear a child, whereas Mary is almost too young and in addition a virgin. The "parent" to whom the angel appears is the father of John, the mother of Jesus. Zechariah's "How?" is taken as a challenge to the angel's veracity, but Mary's as innocent wonder. It is a point of irony that the mature male (a priest having a vision in the temple) is punished for lack of faith, while the young peasant woman believes and is blessed. This foreshadows the theme of reversals in Mary's song.

In addition to the inner connections, this chapter has strong resonances with a number of Old Testament texts. Among them is the Hagar and Sarah story discussed earlier. That story also includes dual pregnancies with one mother elderly and the other young. In both of the stories, the pregnancy upon which the future of God's people depends comes second. But while Sarah treats Hagar cruelly, Elizabeth blesses Mary. Hagar runs from Sarah but returns in time to have her child in the household. Mary runs to Elizabeth but leaves before the birth of the child.

There are also connections between this story and Hannah's giving birth to Samuel (1 Sam. 1:1–2:11). Like Hannah, Elizabeth has been barren throughout her marriage. Also like Hannah, both Elizabeth and Mary will give up their sons to the service of God. The song Hannah sings when Samuel is presented for temple service (1 Sam. 2:1–10) is generally recognized as the pattern for the song of Mary during her visit to Elizabeth.

Elizabeth's response to her pregnancy fits what we know about women's family roles in biblical times. She understands her pregnancy as a sign of divine favor, a removal of the disgrace of barrenness. Yet she shows no hesitance or envy at Mary's greater chosen status.[10]

Mary's response to the angel is more surprising. Although she is very young, she is only "perplexed"—not terrified—at the angel's visit. When he announces that she will bear a child, Mary asks coolly, "How can this be since I am a virgin?" The angel's answer about God's power and Spirit satisfies her. "Here I am, the servant of the Lord; let it be with me according to your word." Mary must be aware that a pregnancy could be her death sentence: since she is engaged, it will be considered proof of adultery, punishable by stoning. Even if she is not put to death, her financial worth (the bride-price her family can expect from her husband) will be reduced. Yet Mary seems to know no fear. When she visits an elderly relative (also pregnant), it is not to escape small-town eyes noticing her swelling body: she stays only until the third month of her pregnancy. Mary's song, celebrating God's pattern of reversing expectations, is full of joy—with no sign of hesitation, let alone fear.

Both Mary and Elizabeth have a grace-filled awareness of divine activity in their lives. Elizabeth's joy makes cultural sense in a way that Mary's does not. Is this because the story lacks verisimilitude, or because her response, like her pregnancy, is miraculous?

Dynamic Analogy. As Mary, why do you run to visit Elizabeth? Are you checking up on the angel's story? Do you need to share your joy? Is there any hesitance at dealing with your family and fiancé? How do you respond when the older woman honors you as "the mother of my Lord"?

As Elizabeth, how does it feel to greet Mary? Are you full of joy, or is there a tinge of sadness at coming in second again? Even after all the years of barrenness, your miracle pregnancy does not receive top billing. Do you regret Mary's departure at the end of three months, or do you urge her to leave before your child is born? As Mary, do you regret missing the birth of John, or are you relieved not to be a part of it?

As Mary or Elizabeth, is your overwhelming sense of your relative one of sisterhood? Do you have a sense of sharing with her in the mighty work of God in the world?

What of the points in your own life when you have had a Mary-or Elizabeth-experience? Perhaps you can recall a time when your neat plans for the future were undone by an unexpected turn of events—a pregnancy, a death, or the loss of a job. Have you been able to experience those surprises as opportunities for grace? Or perhaps you have found yourself surprised by God's grace in your life, only to learn that a friend or relative has a story more amazing than yours. Have you been able to respect her greater joy without denying your own happiness?

Chapter Three

Women and Men
Hermeneutic of Suspicion

"Women and men" is a complex topic in relation to biblical texts. Most biblical texts were written by men, and all biblical texts were transmitted within male-dominated groups. So in a sense, all biblical texts—including those about women—reflect mens' approaches and concerns. And all texts about women, even if they do not mention men directly, are implicitly about women and men. The awareness of human interests playing on the shaping and interpretation of biblical texts leads some readers to apply what is called a 'hermeneutic of suspicion.' A hermeneutic (interpretive method) of suspicion starts from the belief that there may be more to a text than meets the eye. Interpreters who use this method try to discover not only the surface purpose of the text but also any underlying agenda or claim of the text. One question they ask is, *Whose interests are being served?*

This may seem an odd question to ask about biblical texts. The easy answer for those of us who call the Bible "scripture" is that all its texts are inspired: God's interests are being served. On the canonical level, that answer satisfies some. Still, in addition to functioning as part of the canon, these texts have also functioned as part of a social world and a literary world. In those human worlds, whose interests does a given text serve?

One way a biblical text can serve a social agenda is in the characters it chooses to represent as godly and ungodly, righteous and wicked. When the major characters in a text about individuals belong to different social groups, the text may encode an overt dispute between the groups. Another text may seek to reinforce or to undercut the power of a dominant social group.

The social agenda of a biblical text is not always the same as its theological or canonical agenda. To offer a social critique does not necessarily mean calling into question a text's status as scripture. For some interpreters, however, there are texts whose social purpose is so clearly at odds with their understanding of the gospel that they are unwilling to accept the biblical authority of those particular texts. In the end, each interpreter or interpretive community must decide how to deal with difficult texts.

Tamar and Judah: Woman as Righteous Trickster

Read: Genesis 38

The Story. Tamar is married to Er, the oldest of Judah's three sons. But Er is wicked, and Yahweh puts him to death. Judah then assigns Onan, the elder of the two remaining sons, to "perform the duty of a brother-in-law." He evades this duty and is also put to death by Yahweh. Although Judah is now obligated to provide his youngest son, Shelah, as a husband for Tamar, he is afraid that this son will also die. So instead he sends Tamar to her father's house to wait until Shelah is old enough for marriage.

When Shelah is grown, and Tamar realizes that Judah does not intend to fulfill his obligation to her, she takes matters into her own hands. Wearing a veil, she waits at a crossroads for Judah to pass. Judah, now widowed, mistakes her for a prostitute and has sex with her. The agreed price is a kid-goat. As a pledge of payment, Judah leaves his signet, cord, and staff with her. When he sends an agent to make payment and recover the pledge, Tamar is nowhere to be found. Tamar is pregnant, and when her pregnancy becomes obvious, Judah sentences her to be burned. Tamar sends Judah the signet, cord, and staff, along with the message, "It was the owner of these who made me pregnant." Judah then "acknowledged them and said, 'She is more in the right than I, since I did not give her to my son Shelah.'" Judah never has sex with Tamar again. She bears twins, one of whom becomes an ancestor of King David.

Analysis. Judah is one of the twelve sons of Jacob, and the father of the tribe out of which the Davidic dynasty will come. At the beginning of the story, Judah has moved away from his family to Canaanite territory; his wife, the mother of the three sons, is a Canaanite. Although it is not stated in the story that Tamar is also a Canaanite, this is a reasonable inference.

According to later Israelite law, when a married man died and left a childless wife, it was the duty of the dead man's brother (or next-closest available relative) to marry the widow. The first son born of that union would be considered to be the dead man's and would receive his inheritance. A version of this law is presumed in the story. Although the levirate law (the "brother-in-law" law) is designed to preserve the name and inheritance of the deceased man, within the patriarchal system it also functions to protect the widow. With no husband and no male offspring, she is outside the family system. Because Israelite society is based on the extended family, she has marginal social and legal status.[1]

After the death of Onan, Judah sends Tamar back to live in her father's house while waiting for Shelah to become old enough for marriage. We would expect that, as wife of the dead man waiting for marriage to her brother-in-law, she would remain a part of Judah's household rather than returning to her father's domain. Although Judah apparently does not maintain fiscal responsibility for Tamar, he still claims legal authority as head of household to punish her as an adulteress when she becomes pregnant.

The text suggests an ironic attitude toward Judah, the great ancestor. He seems to perceive Tamar as a danger to his family's continuity, while in fact the danger is in his sons' sin and his own unwillingness to fulfill his obligations. Tamar is the one who preserves the family. Although the crossroads where Tamar sits is called the "'opening of the eyes' . . . Judah's vision appears somewhat clouded."[2] In the previous chapter, Judah used the blood of a kid-goat to deceive his father. Now he is himself deceived by the use of a kid-goat as payment.[3] It turns out that a woman who is marginal in numerous ways—childless, widowed, living in the wrong house (her father's, not her husband's), and an apparent jinx to the patriarch's sons—is more righteous than the patriarch himself, the ancestor of the royal dynasty.

The crowning irony in the story comes when Tamar cannot be found, and Judah says, "Let her keep the things as her own, otherwise we will be laughed at." The joke is on Judah, who has been laughed at for thousands of years over this bit of folly.

The chapter as a whole is an interruption in the Joseph story. Joseph has been sold into Egypt, and his story there resumes in chapter 39. Chapter 38 has a meanwhile-back-at-the-ranch effect, serving to mark the passage of time between chapters 37 and 39.

The relationship of this story to its context in the Joseph novella, however, may be greater than this.[4] The irony of the kid-goat has already been noted. Connections with chapter 39 are more direct. In chapter 39, Potiphar's wife attempts to seduce Joseph, although the seduction is not successful, Joseph spends years in jail because she accuses him of attempted rape. In both chapters 38 and 39, one of the sons of Jacob receives sexual advances from a foreign woman who is designated for another man. Judah succumbs, and the result is the continuation of his family line and, eventually, the Davidic dynasty. Unlike Judah, Joseph resists, and he is punished for a time. Judah labels Tamar righteous, whereas Joseph says that Potiphar's wife is tempting him to "great wickedness, and sin against God" (Gen. 39:9).

Because chapter 38 is the interruption, it functions to direct the reading of chapter 39. Without the Tamar and Judah story, it would be possible to read chapter 39 as a characterization of women—particularly foreign women—as evil and dangerous. The story of Tamar and Judah, however, has shown that the danger is not always in the woman. According to this story, a woman's behavior can be righteous rather than wicked, and even a foreign woman's sexual plotting can serve good purposes. The story of Joseph and Potiphar's wife, then, becomes a story of what happened to Joseph, not of what invariably happens. Potiphar's wife is denied the status of Everywoman.

Whose Interests Are Being Served? Because Judah and Tamar together are ancestors of the Davidic line, the story may reflect an interest in the Jerusalem monarchy. Tamar, as a righteous foreign woman, might counter the claim that entanglements with foreign women were destructive of the Davidic kings.

Judah's blindness and folly in the story might on the other hand serve to undercut the authority of the monarchy. In relation to our next story, chapter 38 could function as a north-over-south polemic: Joseph, one of the revered ancestors of the northern realm, is righteous to the point of risking his own well-being, whereas Judah, ancestor of the southern realm's Davidic dynasty, is unjust and has to be tricked into fulfilling his familial obligations.

The chapter also undergirds the levirate law as positive for both men and women. Although this is no doubt true within the Israelite social structure based on male-headed families, the story does not allow for questioning the system that attempted to keep Tamar dependent on the good will of her in-laws.

In addition, the story serves the interests of the marginated members of society, those who do not have the power to claim their rights straightforwardly and so resort to trickster tactics.

Finally, again in counterpoint to the story of Joseph and Potiphar's wife, this story limits ethnic and sexist prejudices, upholding the possibility of female virtue even in a foreigner.

Miriam, Moses, Aaron: Woman as Challenge

Read: Numbers 12

The Story. Having left Egypt, the Israelites are in the wilderness. Miriam and Aaron object to Moses' Cushite wife. They ask, "Has Yahweh spoken only through Moses? Has he not spoken through us also?" Yahweh hears them complaining. At this point the narrator comments, "Now the man Moses was very humble, more so than anyone else on the face of the earth." Then Yahweh calls the three—Moses, Aaron, and Miriam—to the meeting tent and appears in a pillar of cloud. Yahweh upholds Moses' uniqueness: prophets are addressed in visions and dreams, but with Moses Yahweh speaks "mouth to mouth" ("face to face" in the NRSV). Angry, Yahweh departs, and Miriam has become "leprous,[5] as white as snow." Aaron turns and sees her condition and intercedes with Moses, who intercedes with Yahweh, who responds: "If her father had but spit in her face, would she not bear her shame for seven days? Let her be shut out of the camp for seven days." After that time, the people set out on their journey again.

Analysis. There are problems with this story. First, although both Miriam and Aaron challenge Moses, only Miriam is punished with leprosy. And although only Miriam is punished, Aaron's plea begins, "Do not punish *us*." Second, the introduction characterizes the challenge as being based on Moses' marriage to a Cushite, but the quotation of the complaint speaks only of Moses' status in comparison with the other two. Third, the narrator's comment about Moses' humility interrupts the narrative flow and does not contribute to the plot. Fourth, according to the speech of Yahweh, prophets other than Moses receive Yahweh's message through visions and dreams. But according to the surrounding narration, Miriam and Aaron are presented as also hearing the direct word of Yahweh from the divine presence in the pillar of cloud. (This is still one step removed from the claim about Moses: "mouth to mouth"; "he beholds the form of Yahweh.")

These are problems within the text itself. When we move outside the text to examine more of the traditions about Moses, Miriam, and Aaron, there are additional difficulties. The tradition is ambivalent in how it presents Moses' interaction with Yahweh. On the one hand, the claim of this passage that Yahweh speaks directly to Moses is affirmed in Exod. 33:11 (where the Hebrew expression is literally "face to face," and not "mouth to mouth" as in this narrative). On the other hand, this claim is qualified later in the same chapter of Exodus, when Moses is granted a glimpse of Yahweh's form but sees only the back of Yahweh, not the deity's face, because "no one can see me and live" (Exod. 33:23).

Another problem within the larger tradition has to do with the way the roles of Miriam, Moses, and Aaron are remembered. It is quite clear in this text that Yahweh claims Moses as undisputed leader. In the overall shape of the Pentateuch, Moses and Aaron are presented as the two great leaders, Moses as the one who transmitted the divine Torah from Yahweh to the people, and Aaron as the ancestor of the priests of later Israel. We would not be very surprised to find the tradition recording a story of conflict between these two figures. But this story in its final form presents Miriam as the one who is directly punished and thus, we may suppose, the one whose role in the rebellion posed the greater threat. In another strand of biblical tradition, all three are presented as the great ancestral leaders of the Israelites (Micah 6:4). And elsewhere in the Pentateuch Miriam is labeled a prophet (Exod. 15:20). Miriam is also one of very few women included in a census list in Numbers (26:59) and in a genealogical list of Israelite ancestry (1 Chron. 6:3). In fact, she is the only woman who is there in her own right and not as someone's wife or mother.

What are we to make of these difficulties? The consensus among interpreters is that the first group of difficulties is caused by the conflation of two different stories of challenges to Moses' authority.

The first, by Miriam, involved his marriage to a Cushite and was punished by leprosy; the second, by both Miriam and Aaron, involved the question of sole or shared authority. If a punishment was connected with that story, it is not preserved.[6] This division into sources is possible. Whatever the sources for the narrative, though, it is interesting that the story came out in this particular way, so that both Miriam and Aaron offer a double challenge to Moses but only Miriam is punished. Aaron, in fact, is apparently acting within his priestly role when he turns toward Miriam and sees her skin condition. It is the role of the priest to diagnose such ailments and, when appropriate, impose or lift a quarantine.[7]

We may suspect that the transmitters of the tradition had trouble with this text and with the stories that lay behind it. The problems and gaps in this text—and between this text and other elements of the tradition—suggest some anxiety about the roles of the three leaders. It is likely that Miriam is a greater leader than the later tradition admits. Rita Burns places Miriam in the cultic sphere (thus the association with Aaron).[8] The tradition remembers Miriam as one of the great leaders of the wilderness period but does not record much about what she actually did as leader.[9] Perhaps the later tradition is not able to ascribe to a woman the roles in which Miriam acted.

Within this text we must ask, *What about Moses' Cushite wife? Is she a real issue in the text?* The reference to the wife seems to work in at least two directions. On the one hand, she is a foreigner, and Aaron and Miriam's negative reaction may express a long-standing concern about the foreign woman as dangerous to the Israelite man and Israelite society in general. In this text, though, the foreign woman seems to be only a pretext for the rebellion: the real issue is the exclusiveness of Moses' authority. This leaves Moses' marriage functionally approved by the narrator without requiring Yahweh to say explicitly that it is legitimate to have a foreign wife. So, on the one hand the text works against the anti-foreign agenda of some strains of the tradition, while on the other hand it is passive in its resistance.

There may also be a subtle play on the wife's race or skin color in the text. Moses' wife is presented explicitly as a Cushite—which is to say, a black African.[10] We may suppose that her skin is darker than that of most Israelites. Miriam's punishment involves her skin turning "white as snow." Surely some irony is present.

But the biggest problem in the final form of the text is that the rebellion is presented as that of Miriam and Aaron, but the punishment is directed at Miriam only. Commentators have offered several possible explanations. One is that suffering from an unclean disease, which would render a person unfit for priestly service, would be unthinkable for Aaron, the archetypal priest, and would upset the balance of power and authority between him and Moses.[11] But of course it would have been possible to describe another punishment for Aaron that would not compromise his priestly purity. Another explanation has to do with roles in later tradition. In time, Moses became associated with the legal materials in the Pentateuch, and also, because of the tradition about his special relationship with Yahweh, he was known as the forerunner of the intermediaries who would later be called prophets. And Aaron became known as the ancestor of the Jerusalem priesthood. But Miriam's authority is not similarly preserved. No authoritative group looks back on Miriam as their founding mother. It is possible, then, that because this story was edited over the generations, there were some who had an interest in the portrayal of Moses and others with an interest in the portrayal of Aaron, but no one with a hand in the editing had an interest in the positive portrayal of Miriam. She thus became the one who could be portrayed as under divine punishment without stepping on any later toes. Phyllis Trible suggests a less innocent interpretation, speaking of a "vendetta against Miriam" and "the threat that she represented to . . . early Israel."[12]

Whose Interests Are Being Served? Moses' interests and the interests of those who understood their authority to derive from his are supported most strongly. Aaron's interests are limited but not denied: he remains in his priestly role although subordinated to Moses. Even the interests of the Cushite woman who had married Moses, and thus the interests of those who argued for Israelite openness to foreigners, are supported. Everyone's interests except Miriam's seem to receive some support.

In its final form, the narrative leaves us with the message that it is not a good thing for either men or women to rebel against the power structure, but it is a particularly dangerous thing for women.

When she is stricken with the skin disease, Miriam does not speak at all. It takes Aaron's intercession with Moses, Moses' subsequent intercession with Yahweh, and a week of penance before Miriam is readmitted to the community. Note too that the justification for her punishment (which the text attributes to Yahweh) generalizes her humiliation by reminding all women of their subordinate social place: "If her father had but spit in her face, would she not bear her shame for seven days?"

Looking at the Miriam texts as a group, we may ask why, if Miriam was in early times considered a great leader, did the tradition come so close to forgetting her? My guess is that this is one result of the increasing male domination of Israelite society under the monarchy and later. Early Israel may have been open to leaders of both genders, but as women were increasingly marginalized, the tradition conveniently forgot the women leaders among their ancestors.

David and Bathsheba: Woman as Prop in a Man's Story

Read: 2 Samuel 11–12
The Story. David, king of Israel, is at home while his army is out fighting a battle. He sees Bathsheba bathing nearby. She is the wife of a Hittite named Uriah, but Israelite enough to purify herself after her monthly period. When David sees her, he wants her, sends for her, and has sex with her. Later she sends word that she has become pregnant, and David has Uriah brought home from the battlefront in an attempt to trick him into thinking the child is legitimate. The plan fails. Uriah hints at the regulations governing holy war—which include abstinence from sex—and does not even sleep in his own house. Then David arranges for Uriah to be killed in battle, after which he marries Bathsheba and she gives birth to a son.

Yahweh is displeased and sends Nathan the prophet to David. Nathan tells a story about a rich man who, rather than killing his own livestock to feed a guest, seizes the only lamb of a poor man. When David expresses righteous outrage at the rich man's injustice and lack of compassion, Nathan tells him, "You are the man!" Nathan announces David's punishment—trouble in his household. David repents. Nathan says that Yahweh will forgive him, but the baby will die.

When the baby becomes ill, David fasts and pleads with God. After the child dies, David resumes normal life—to the astonishment of his servants. David's reasoning is: "While the child was still alive, I fasted and wept; for I said, 'Who knows? Yahweh may be gracious to me, and the child may live.' But now he is dead; why should I fast? Can I bring him back again?"

David consoles Bathsheba and has sex with her. She bears a son, whom David names Solomon.

Analysis. Bathsheba is the fourth of David's wives. Earlier he married Michal, the daughter of Saul (whom Saul later gives to another man in marriage); Abigail, who is the wife of Nabal when David meets her; and Ahinoam, who is not further identified, although there are hints that she may have been a widow of Saul.[13] Later wives are mentioned, but there are no stories about them.

In spite of its content, this story is only minimally about women and men. The narrator does not tell us about Bathsheba's feelings. In the context of the story, they do not matter. Bathsheba is not a full character but only a prop in the story of David. Characters include David, Uriah, and Nathan, but Bathsheba is really not a character at all. We cannot tell from the narrative whether she is bathing on the roof in order to attract the king's attention, or whether she is innocent or, at worst, unthinking. She could be a seductress, a rape victim, or someone between these two extremes. We do not know how she reacts to the death of Uriah, whether she is pleased to marry the king, or even how much she grieves the death of her son.

It is common for biblical narratives to include characters who function only as props. That seems surprising in this story, because the woman is essential to the story. But it is important to be aware that the story does not ascribe motives to her. And it is also important to recognize that women are not the only ones to serve as props in other people's stories. We might say the same of Ishmael, Isaac, and perhaps Abraham in the story of Sarah and Hagar. Biblical narrative tolerates only a few full characters in any scene.

David's reign is narrated not only here but also in 1 Chronicles. The Chronicles versions, however, does not tell this story. It includes an account of the taking of Rabbah (1 Chron. 20) which does not mention Uriah or Bathsheba. David does displease Yahweh in the following chapter, but there his sin is taking a census. Chronicles never even uses the name Bathsheba, although it does apparently indicate the same character by using the name Bathshua; she is mentioned only in a list of David's sons (1 Chron. 3:5). Uriah's name occurs only in a list of warriors (1 Chron. 11:41).

Bathsheba later becomes a powerful figure in the royal court. She takes an active role in the discussion of who will succeed David and acts as adviser to Solomon while he is king. This suggests that the queen mother is a more powerful role in Judah than the king's wife.[14] In addition to being a queen mother, Bathsheba is the dynastic mother,[15] ancestor with David of the entire dynasty of the southern realm.

If this were a chapter about men and men, it would be interesting to speculate about Uriah. His choices play significant parts in the plot, but it is not clear whether he makes those choices innocently or calculates them. Does he suspect or know that David has impregnated Bathsheba? Is he in some sense playing with the king? If he is the trickster, his games bring about his own death. Or is he, although a Hittite, a righteous Yahwist, while David, founder of the dynasty and beloved of God, is adulterer and murderer?

Whose Interests Are Being Served? This story can serve the interests of a number of groups. Assuming that it is an early story, written around or shortly after the time when David's successor was chosen, the story could work to discredit the sons of Bathsheba. Alternatively, it could serve the interests of Solomon by debunking the idea that he was the product of adultery: no, that child is dead; Solomon is conceived after his parents are legally married. These two opposing possibilities exist because we do not have access to the Jerusalem gossip at the time of the succession. How much of the story was common knowledge and how much would have been new to its audience?

This story and others like it also serve the interests of prophets, especially as advisers in the royal court. In these stories, the prophet brings the word, the king listens, and although there is punishment, life turns out all right (that is, as long as you don't think too much about the dead baby).

Because the righteousness of Uriah the Hittite is shown to be greater than that of David, God's favorite Israelite, the text could also support the interests of those who want Israel to be open to outsiders. Bathsheba's interests are not a factor in this story.

The interpretation of the story can also be used to serve a variety of interests. Because Bathsheba's feelings and motives are not described, it is tempting to read them into the text in a way that suits the interpreter's own motives. It is possible to read her as a willing adulteress, even a temptress, and to find wantonness in her decision to bathe on the roof. It is equally possible to see her as a rape victim and to find the story a cautionary tale about men's abuse of power over women. Careful readers will be suspicious of both of these kinds of readings. Any interpreter who reads motives into Bathsheba's behavior is writing a new story, not simply reading this one, and should be open to alternate readings.

The narrative reinforces the notion that the person who counts in a family is the male head of household, that others are important only as they relate to him. As Bathsheba is a non-character, so is the infant son born to her and David: his death is David's punishment.

The Widow of Zarephath: Woman Saving/ Being Saved by a Prophet

Read: 1 Kings 17:8–16
The Story. During a drought, Yahweh sends Elijah to a widow at Zarephath in Sidon. The widow is gathering firewood to use in preparing the last of her food (a little meal and oil) for herself and her son. Elijah asks first for water, and she is about to get for him when he asks also for bread. She turns him down. This small amount of food is all she has, and after this meal she and her son will starve to death. Elijah insists that if she feeds him first, Yahweh will then provide enough for her and her son. Elijah promises that if she does as he asks, the food will last until the rain returns. The woman complies. It turns out that he has been telling the truth: the food does last throughout the drought.

Analysis. Elijah is a prophet of the northern realm during the ninth century not long after the breakdown of the Davidic confederation. (Israel and Judah have become separate realms.) Ahab is king, and his wife, Jezebel, is a Canaanite princess, daughter of the king of Sidon (the same Sidon which controls Zarephath, home of the widow that Elijah visits).

This is the second of three scenes in this chapter, all of which are connected to a drought proclaimed by Elijah throughout the region. In the first scene, Elijah has been fed by ravens along a stream which has since dried up. In the third scene, which contains the characters from this one, the widow's son will die, and Elijah will resuscitate him. All three scenes of this chapter build toward Elijah's confrontation with the prophets of Baal in chapter 18.

In this story, the widow's behavior is striking. It is surprising not that she refuses the first request from the stranger to share her food, but that she succumbs to his insistence, based on a promise that she will have enough for herself and her son. She is apparently not a worshiper of Yahweh, whom she refers to as "Yahweh *your* God" (emphasis added). And yet, according to the text, Yahweh has commanded her to feed Elijah (although it is not clear that she knows this), and she does. In accord with the promise, the food lasts.

How is one to read Elijah's initial request for water, then food? Richard Nelson finds it "a roundabout request, almost painfully polite," which places the widow between "the demands of ancient hospitality and the harsh reality of famine."[16] As I read the encounter, though, Elijah's almost casual demand, as if he can requisition as an afterthought the woman's only means of survival for herself and her son, comes across as almost brutally arrogant.

In the larger book context, Elijah as a prophet of Yahweh has significant power, and the woman (a widow, cut off from the extended-family system on which social rights depend) has virtually none. In the first scene of the story itself, the woman has some power that Elijah does not: she controls the food. He has to persuade her to feed him first. The boy has no power at all. In this story, the characters are Elijah and the unnamed widow, and the boy is only a prop. Even within this story, Elijah has greater power through prophetic access to the power of Yahweh, which is presented as absolute. But he does not have recognized social power. He has embarked on a campaign in opposition to Ahab and Jezebel, and so he is in the process of making himself an outlaw. In 19:2 Jezebel will take an oath to have him killed.

Whose Interests Are Being Served? The story promotes the interests of Elijah and, above all, the interests of Yahwism over Baalism. More generally, it promotes the interests of prophets over rulers.

This prophet-over-ruler dynamic is different from what we saw in the previous story. Nathan was an accepted member of the royal court; Elijah will come under the death sentence of the queen. Both prophets offer critiques of behavior in the royal court, but Nathan's critique of David is accepted, whereas Elijah's critique of Ahab and Jezebel is not.

Although Baal is a storm god connected with the fertility of the land, in this story it is Yahweh (through the prophet) who is responsible for the drought (and later for its end). The geographical setting of the story (Sidon, Jezebel's home region and clearly Baal territory) makes a further Yahwistic point. Yahweh's power is doubly expanded: Yahweh is able to control Baal's area of competence in Baal country, both through nature (the drought) and through suspension of natural processes (the miracle of the oil and grain).

While Jezebel is a paradigm of the dangerous foreign woman, this widow is also a non-Israelite woman. It is to her and not to an Israelite that Yahweh sends Elijah. She becomes the instrument of Elijah's salvation, then he of hers and her son's. The pattern here parallels that of the Tamar and Judah story in that it is a positive story about a socially powerless foreign woman inserted into a negative story about a socially powerful foreign woman. Perhaps there is a double message here. Positively, not all foreign women are Jezebels, but negatively, foreign women with power are seen as dangerous.

According to Luke, Jesus also notes the oddity of the use of a foreign woman in this story: "But the truth is, there were many widows in Israel in the time of Elijah . . . yet Elijah was sent to none of them except to a widow at Zarephath in Sidon" (Luke 4:25–26). It is after he gave this and another example of God saving a foreigner (Naaman) that the people of Nazareth are ready to kill him. Apparently the people recognized that this story, or at least Jesus' use of it, did not serve their interests. It seemed wrong to them to highlight a story in which Israelites were not the ones chosen and blessed.

Women, the Eleven, and the Evangelist: Women's Voices Ignored

Read: Luke 24:1-12

The Story. It is early the morning of the Sunday after Jesus' crucifixion. A group of women take spices to the tomb to give Jesus a belated proper burial (the Sabbath had prevented them from doing so when he was first buried). They find the tomb but no body. Perplexed, they are confronted by "two men in dazzling clothes" who ask them, "Why do you look for the living among the dead? He is not here but has risen. Remember how he told you while he was still in Galilee, that the Son of Man must be handed over to sinners, and be crucified, and on the third day rise again." Then they remember and go to tell "the eleven and to all the rest." Finally, some of the women are identified by name: "Mary Magdalene, Joanna, Mary the mother of James, and the other women with them." The apostles do not believe the women, whose words "seemed to them an idle tale" (Luke 24:11).

Analysis. In all four gospels, women are present at Jesus' tomb on Easter morning, but there are similarities and differences among the versions. How many women are present? Who are they? Do they see only the empty tomb, or also one or two angels, or Jesus?

Although Luke's version does not have very many unique elements, two are significant. First, this is the only one of the four gospels in which the women present are not commissioned, either by the angel(s) or by Jesus, to go and tell the other disciples what they have seen and/or heard. Second, it is the only account in which it is explicitly said that the others do not believe the message of the women.[17] In fact, the women's words seem to them "an idle tale."

In Matthew and Mark, the women are the only witnesses to the empty tomb. Both Luke and John have Peter go to the tomb and verify that it is empty. (In John, the beloved disciple accompanies Peter.) Neither Luke nor Mark includes an Easter morning appearance of Jesus to a woman.[18] Luke does, however, include two other appearances later on Easter, without explicitly stating that women are present.

Pheme Perkins distinguishes between "two narrative traditions associated with Easter: (a) the empty tomb and (b) appearances of the Lord."[19] The empty tomb is the physical evidence that the crucifixion of Jesus did not end his story. But without the proclamation of the Resurrection, there is no Easter faith and no possibility of the Christian church.

Linking these two traditions, of empty tomb and appearances of the risen Lord, are the accounts of angel appearances, by means of which the "resurrection kerygma was introduced into the tomb tradition."[20] Perkins believes that the discovery of the empty tomb by women is historical, and that, as suggested by the angel narratives, women were "the first to hear the Easter message."[21] Because she understands Matthew's and John's narratives to be independent of each other, she also suspects an underlying early tradition of an Easter morning appearance to a woman.[22]

The tradition that women are the ones first entrusted with the Easter message provides a challenge to the early church. Women are not allowed to give legal testimony in either Jewish or Roman law. Thus, the earliest witnesses to the resurrection proclamation are not legally credible. This may help explain why the tradition is anxious to get men to the tomb (Peter in Luke 24:12; Peter and the beloved disciple in John 20:3-10) and to emphasize the appearances to men. If the church's proclamation were to depend on the testimony of women, would not all the world suspect (as Luke claims that the apostles did) that the resurrection narratives are just "idle tales"?

Luke's attitude toward women, hailed by some feminists as liberated, is condemned by others as restrictive.[23] On the one hand, Luke includes far more stories about women than do the other gospels. But on the other hand, women are portrayed primarily in passive roles.[24] According to Mary Rose D'Angelo: "Women speak in the Gospel [of Luke] only to be corrected by Jesus."[25] She concludes that the author of Luke has two purposes in the inclusion and treatment of stories about women. First, there is a need for stories about women to use in the catechesis of women Christians. But second, there is also a desire that these women confine their behavior to passive roles that will not challenge the ideology of imperial Rome.

Whose Interests Are Being Served? On first reading, one might suppose that the story serves the interests of women: women are the ones faithful enough to go to Jesus' tomb to give him a proper burial, and women are the ones first given the message of the resurrection.

On closer examination, though, the story serves the interests of those who would like to keep women quiet and passive in the church. These women are not given the commission to proclaim Jesus' Resurrection. When they share the news anyway, their proclamation is considered "idle talk" by the men (and women?) to whom they speak.

When we continue to ponder the story, however, we may revert to something like the first reading. The story may explicitly tell us that women's testimony is ignored, and yet the testimony of these women has endured for nearly two thousand years. Far from being "idle tales," the women's story has helped to shape the church.

This is a story to which the silenced (women or men) may turn for encouragement when others think them to be telling "idle tales" as they recount their own experiences or the words of angels. As D'Angelo concludes, "Like many another Christian author, Luke may have reckoned without the subversive potential of telling women about themselves."[26]

Priscilla, Aquila, Apollos: Woman as Partner in the Gospel

Read: Acts 18:1-3, 18-19, 24-28
The Story. Aquila and Priscilla are a Christian couple in Corinth, refugees from Rome "because Claudius had ordered all Jews to leave Rome." Paul stays with them, and the three, all tentmakers, work together.

When Paul goes to Syria, Priscilla and Aquila accompany him. They remain in Ephesus, but after a discussion in the synagogue, Paul goes on.

A Christian Alexandrian Jew named Apollos comes to Ephesus and, although he speaks "with burning enthusiasm" and teaches accurately "the things concerning Jesus," he knows only the baptism of John. So when he speaks in the synagogue, Priscilla and Aquila explain "the Way of God to him more accurately." After this, Apollos is an eloquent speaker.

Analysis. Priscilla and Aquila are also mentioned (with Prisca instead of Priscilla) in Romans 16:3, 1 Cor. 16:19, and 2 Tim. 4:19. Interpreters note that, although the introduction of the couple lists them as "Aquila and Priscilla" (with the man's name first), most references are to "Priscilla (or Prisca) and Aquila." This seems to reflect Priscilla as the leading figure in the pair. Yet the two are always listed together, and there is no hint of rivalry between them.

Acts is connected with Luke as the second of a two-part work showing the spread of Christianity throughout the Roman empire. The author generally speaks in terms that will be acceptable in the ideology of the empire, where women's increasing freedom is under attack.

In recent years, feminist interpreters have questioned Acts' depiction of women's ministries: "By stressing their status as prominent and wealthy, the author neglects their contribution as missionaries and leaders of churches in their own right."[27] Tabitha/ Dorcas (a philanthropist who provides clothes for the women of Joppa in Acts 9:36-43) is the only woman in Acts called a "disciple" (Greek *mathetria*). She is not, however, called a minister, although men providing for widows receive that label.[28] Tabitha is the object of a miracle raising: the widows are understandably distressed at her death. Lydia (Acts 16:14-15, 40), a merchant and the first European Christian, is the owner of a house in which a congregation meets: "Acts 16:40 suggests that Lydia's house quickly became a center of the Philippian church, but Luke does not credit Lydia with any leadership role in that development."[29]

Thus it is striking that Priscilla and Aquila appear as a missionary and teaching pair (although no formal titles are used), who travel with Paul from Corinth to Ephesus and correct the doctrine of Apollos, a prominent and dynamic leader of the early church.

Whose Interests Are Being Served? Why is Priscilla mentioned here? Is she such a prominent figure that she cannot be ignored? Is this one reference to a woman leader in ministry a tokenistic attempt to cover an otherwise noticeable lack?

Chapter 18 of Acts is clearly intended to support Paul, the focus figure in the latter part of the book. Because there appears to be some tension between followers of Apollos and those of Paul (see 1 Cor. 3), and because Acts attempts to portray the early church as free of serious dissension, it might help the author's cause to minimize Apollos' authority and credibility. Choosing precisely this situation to highlight a woman's ministry might be Luke's way of attempting to reduce Apollos as a true leader figure within the church.

Intentionally or not, though, Luke's depiction of Priscilla and Aquila serves as a model for women and men in cooperative ministry.

Chapter Four

Women and Jesus
Reading from Below

Christian Feminists and Jesus

Christians perceptions of Jesus are framed by the double claim of the incarnation. In one person, Jesus, Christians find both a unique revelation of God's own self and at the same time a fully human being. There are points of both continuity and difference between understandings of Jesus as the son of God and Jesus as a first-century Jewish man.

This double claim can be complicating for Christians who are feminists. As Christians we may want to trust Jesus fully as Christ and son of God. Yet as feminists we may find ourselves hesitant with him as a man and suspicious of other men's representations of him.

What does it mean to affirm that Jesus was not only God's self-revelation but also a fully human being? Can we take seriously the Gospel claim that there are some things that "not even the son of man" knows? Can we imagine Jesus learning and growing as humans do? Understanding Jesus as having human limitations is one way of taking the incarnation seriously: during Jesus' lifetime, God the son was not a God who happened to look and sound and bleed like a man, but he really was a man.

For this chapter, I would like to make our first question that of how gospel stories show the man Jesus relating to women. This can have an effect on how we relate to Jesus spiritually, but I would like the starting place to be ancient relationships and for implications about relationships in our own time to come out of our understanding of the ancient ones.

This is not meant to diminish the importance of these stories and the relationships they reflect for faith today. If we find ourselves arguing with Jesus, we may feel that we are overly bold, even in dangerous territory. Yet I urge you (and myself) not to begin with rules about what we can allow ourselves to think or feel. Rather, let us try first to identify our reactions honestly and then to reflect on them as they are. Maybe we will end up entirely affirming the relationship with Jesus we had before, or maybe that relationship will change. We'll never know if we don't give it the opportunity to grow and change.

There is a wide range of ways feminists talk about Jesus and ways that Jesus fits into the faith of feminists. Some idealize him. Some consider him to be the "only feminist man" ever, or at least in his culture. Some imagine what it would have been like if he had been a woman instead of a man. Certainly, Jesus' way of relating to women was unusual within his culture—and remains so in ours. In this chapter, we will try to discover what is special and valuable in his attitude without denying his humanity and the fact that he belonged to his own culture.

There are several dangers of idealizing Jesus. One is that we may reject his culture and adopt anti-Jewish attitudes.[1] If everything good about Jesus is defined in contrast to the people around him, we may be tempted to find nothing good in Judaism. On the other hand, it is equally possible (and, I think, more realistic) to see Jesus as a realization of the potential within his culture. Because Jesus was a Jew, his treatment of women represents a possibility within Judaism rather than a contrast with Judaism.

Another danger of idealizing Jesus is that we may let other men off the hook. Jesus, we may say, was special in a way that other men cannot be, and so we might excuse the sexism of our own fathers, husbands, brothers, sons, colleagues, bosses, or employees. Because Jesus was a real man, his best relationships with women reflect possibilities for all men.

Our attempts to deal with Jesus the man are complicated by the fact that we know about Jesus' activities almost exclusively from stories in the gospels. We have a very incomplete picture of Jesus' relationships with women, one that is filtered through the concerns of the (male) evangelists and other shapers of the tradition. Thus, at times when we think we are responding to Jesus, we may actually be reacting to the way that the gospel writers presented him.

Reading from Below

Reading from below is a liberation strategy developed in Latin American base communities. It means reading from the point of view of the least privileged person or group in the text, and it is best done by those in our own world who identify with 'the least' in the text. This makes it a difficult strategy for people in positions of power or dominance in the culture. Sometimes one can read as 'the least' simply by reading as a woman, but more often 'the least' also occurs in regard to other factors such as class, race, and age. I attempt this strategy because I believe it is important, but also with the awareness that my efforts are certain to be inadequate. Thus, I also rely on the readings of people who can identify in other ways with 'the least' in the text.

Reading from below is based on the belief that, throughout the Bible, God shows a special concern for society's least privileged members. The Israelites remember their ancestors as being slaves in Egypt who were liberated by Yahweh. They remember their judges as including a woman, an illegitimate man, and a left-handed man. They remember the great dynasty of David as beginning with the youngest son of a shepherd family. They remember the prophets as including men and women from various social classes and occupations, many of whom express special concern for the poor and oppressed in their own society. This tendency continues in Jesus, who is neither rich nor privileged.

Jesus also lives out the preference for the poor and dispossessed. It is apparent that in his ministry Jesus did associate with and honor people who were considered unacceptable in segments of his own society. Thus, reading from below can highlight some of Jesus' own concerns. Finally, the early church was a community that welcomed and empowered outcasts, so reading from below can also emphasize important issues in early Christianity.

The Samaritan Woman at the Well

Read: John 4

The Story. Jesus and the disciples walk through Samaria. The disciples leave Jesus at a town well and go in search of food. A woman

comes to draw water, and Jesus asks for some. The woman is
surprised. Jesus begins to talk about offering her "living water,"
after which she will never thirst again. She does not understand.
Although he is speaking metaphorically, she insists on taking his
words literally. Jesus acknowledges the woman's past life: "You
have had five husbands, and the one you have now is not your
husband." She is impressed enough to consider him a prophet and
begins probing on religious issues, particularly the differences
between Jews and Samaritans. Is Jerusalem or Gerizim the right
place to worship? While affirming Judaism ("Salvation is of the
Jews"), Jesus points to a future in which neither Jerusalem nor
Gerizim will be needed. When the woman mentions the hope for
the Messiah, shared by Jews and Samaritans, Jesus says, "The one
who speaks to you is he." The woman runs to tell the townsfolk
about the man "who told me everything I ever did."

Meanwhile, the disciples come back and show that they are as
unable to understand Jesus' talk about food as the woman had
been to understand his talk about drink. Samaritans come and urge
him to stay, and he does for two days.

Analysis. In Roman times, the province of Samaria was inhabited
by people who were not Jews, although their religion had features
in common with Judaism as it was developing. The Samaritans
identified themselves as worshipers of the God of the Bible, but not
in the same way that the Jews did. And so there were conflicts
between Jews and Samaritans.

Many of Jesus' people avoided all contact with Samaritans. In
this story, Jesus did not: he and his disciples walked through
Samaria, and Jesus even spoke to a Samaritan woman. His behavior was doubly objectionable—first because he was dealing with a
Samaritan, and second because he was talking publicly with a
strange woman.[2] The woman's sex, ethnic background, and
religion, then, all made his approach to her at least questionable if
not illegal.

The conversation about living water is an example of missed
communication. Jesus is speaking symbolically; the woman is
interpreting his words concretely. This is typical of John's strategy
and is used not only with foreigners and women. In the preceding
chapter, Nicodemus, a member of the religious establishment, is
just as dense. We see equal folly among the disciples at the end of

this story, when Jesus speaks of being nourished from sources the disciples do not know, and they wonder who has given him food. Jesus deals with the woman as she is. He acknowledges her past (she has had five husbands, and is living with a man to whom she is not married) but does not judge her. In his awareness of her life's details, Jesus is presented as having supernatural, or at least unusual, knowledge. Jesus' hint that he is the Messiah is the first time in the Gospel of John that he suggests such a claim.

Reading from Below. This Samaritan is a woman outside the boundaries of acceptable society. She is not Jewish, and she is neither married nor living in her father's house, but with a man not her husband. There is no mention of children, and it is likely that she has none, or at least no adult children in whose households she could live in instead of relying on a man not her husband.

Although the woman does not understand what Jesus says, she is moved by both his display of knowledge about her and his claim about who he is. She is persuaded enough of Jesus' uniqueness to witness to others. To later readers she may appear slow to understand, but compared with many characters in John's Gospel, she is very quick to accept Jesus. She becomes one of the first evangelists, hurrying to tell others about this man, asking, "Can this be the Messiah?" John thus shows a person who is 'the least' in regard to sex, ethnicity, religion, and social position being chosen by and responding to Jesus.

The text suggests that the woman shares society's low opinion of herself. After Jesus tells her about her marital history, she tells the townspeople, "Come and see a man who told me everything I have ever done." In the woman's own eyes, her life is nothing but a series of marriages that has left her without a husband.

Later tradition focuses on the woman's living arrangement and depicts her as a woman lacking in moral standards. It is more likely that she is a woman lacking options. She has been married, but her husband died or divorced her. She married again, and again death or divorce left her alone. She apparently has outlived or been divorced by five husbands. She has no place in society, which probably means both no adult children and no one left in the most recent husband's family to support her. Now she is living with a man who has not married her. In a small town, how else could she live? In a city, perhaps she might support herself through taking up a craft of some sort, but this is not an option in a village such as Sychar. Perhaps the only way she could support herself in such a village is by prostitution. She chooses instead to live with a man to whom she is not married. This is not considered honorable in her society, but she does not have an honorable option.

What does the woman gain from the encounter with Jesus? In physical terms, she receives nothing. Jesus has no intention of alleviating her physical thirst, of saving her from the daily walk to and from the well. He neither tells her to leave the man with whom she is living nor approves of her living arrangement. He does not tell her it is all right for her to worship on Gerizim, although he does say that even Jerusalem worship was temporary.

Yet the woman gains something from the encounter. She becomes excited about Jesus and the possibility that he is the Messiah. A woman who understands her life to consist of a past of grief and rejection and a present of shame catches a vision of future hope.

To read this story from below, imagine a woman in our own setting who is caught in a life that our society considers dishonorable, connected with a religion that is not quite orthodox. What does Jesus say to her? How does she respond? How does she share her understanding of Jesus with her friends and neighbors? What does the encounter with Jesus mean for her future?

A Woman Caught in Adultery

Read: John 7:53–8:11

The Story. Jesus is in the temple, sitting and teaching. The authorities bring to him a woman who has been caught in adultery. They say to him, "Teacher, this woman was caught in the very act of committing adultery. Now in the law Moses commanded us to stone such women. Now what do you say?" This is identified by the narrator as a test, an attempt to find a charge to bring against Jesus.

Jesus bends down and writes with his finger on the ground. He straightens up and says, "Let anyone among you who is without sin be the first to throw a stone at her." Then he bends down and writes some more. One by one, beginning with the elders, they leave, until only Jesus and the woman are left. Jesus stands and says to her: "Woman, where are they? Has no one condemned you?" At her "No one, sir," he says, "Neither do I condemn you. Go your way, and from now on do not sin again."

Analysis. Some of the earliest manuscripts of John do not include this story, and it seems to many interpreters disruptive in its context. The NRSV, therefore, encloses it in double brackets, to suggest that it is not in place here.

By sitting in the temple and teaching, Jesus is claiming religious authority. Sitting was the posture for authoritative religious teaching; the temple was the place of religious authority. So the official authorities test his authority.

These religious leaders want Jesus to pronounce a legal decision: what should be done to this woman? There is no right answer that Jesus can give. He is known to consort with "sinners." To condemn the woman to death would be condemning his own lifestyle, yet refusing to do so would imply declaring the law of Moses invalid.

Jesus does neither. Instead, he bends down and twice writes on the ground. What is the importance of this? It is common to ask what he is writing. Interpreters who take this approach imagine that Jesus writes the sins of each of the accusers. It is when they realize their own guilt before the law that they walk away. (In fact, some manuscripts add this interpretation to the text.)

Yet the most reliable texts do not say what Jesus is writing; and so this interpretation is a guess, a plausible but not absolute way of filling in the gap in the text. Because the text does not tell us, what Jesus is writing may not be the point. The point is rather likely to be that he is writing with his finger on the ground. By doing so, he refuses to fall into the authorities' trap and make a decision which they are determined to find wrong; instead, he changes the issue.

One by one, the accusers leave. Is it because they are convicted of guilt? Is it because they recognize Jesus' authority? Is it because they know they have lost this round and want to begin planning the next? Again, the text is open.

Jesus does not investigate the charges and declare the woman legally guilty or innocent. His concern is not with the woman's past but with her future.

Reading from Below. The woman is not a character. Like Bathsheba with David, she is a prop in a story in which she deserves to be a main character. What does she think? How does she feel? Is she purely grateful to Jesus, or does a part of her resent his power? The text does not say.

By refusing to condemn the woman, Jesus refuses to make her a scapegoat—but neither does he approve her behavior. He also refuses to make sexual sin greater than any other. Gail O'Day points out that Jesus hints at the past sins of the scribes and Pharisees and warns against future sins of the woman. It is not as though she is a sinner while the rest of them are not; all are sinners. All are offered a new future.[3]

In our own society, as in that of Jesus, it is common to judge sexual behavior more harshly than any other. The least for this text are those who are ostracized by a sinful society for sexual reasons, especially when they are also legally powerless. For those of us who identify with the righteous accusers, Jesus' words remind us that the accused are no less human, are no different from the rest of us. Even the least belong to God.

Who are the sexual sinners in our society? Imagine the encounter with Jesus as they might experience it. How would it feel to hear him suggest that the accusers are also guilty? How could they respond when he says, "Go and sin no more?" Where do they go? How are their lives changed?

The Canaanite Woman

Read: Matthew 15:21-28

The Story. Jesus is in the coastal region of Tyre and Sidon. A woman approaches and asks him to perform an exorcism on her daughter. He does not even answer. The disciples ask him to send her away. He says, "I am not sent except to the lost sheep of the house of Israel." She kneels, pleads. He says, "It is not fair to take the children's bread and throw it to the dogs." The woman says, "Yes, Lord, yet even the dogs eat the crumbs that fall from their masters' table." Finally Jesus responds: "Woman, great is your faith! Let it be done for you as you wish." The girl is healed instantly.

Analysis. Tyre and Sidon are outside Jewish territory. These cities were historically settled by the sea peoples, who are unrelated ethnically to the Jews.

The story (which occurs in similar form in Mark 7:24–30) is not an easy one. It presents a view of Jesus different from that of stories in which he is open and accepting toward outsiders. This time, when a foreign woman approaches Jesus, he first ignores her, then insults her. It takes perseverance on her part before he responds to her need and heals the daughter.

The easiest way for some Christians to interpret this story is to see Jesus as testing the woman. If this is the case, his apparent harshness is really a way of encouraging the woman to express her faith. Yet there is nothing in the story that tells us to interpret it in this way, and to do so requires believing that Jesus deliberately tried to sound less open than in fact he was.

It is also possible to understand the story as a straightforward dialogue in which Jesus and the women are honest with each other throughout. Some may find the questions raised by this reading difficult. Could it be that Jesus had the grace to be taught by a woman, a foreigner? Could it be that this stranger with the possessed daughter was the first to challenge Jesus in a way that he could see was right?[4]

Personally, I prefer this second reading. I like the thought that this encounter did open Jesus' eyes, that he was compassionate enough to see that his prejudices against non-Jews were unfair. I have more respect for Jesus the man thinking he could learn from this foreign woman than thinking he was tormenting her deliberately in order to make a show of her faith.

What a contrast to the story of the Samaritan woman! In that story, Jesus reached out to the woman. In this story, the woman must be tenacious.

Reading from Below. Who are those who are told today that they do not belong among the people of God, that the life and healing of the gospel are not for the likes of them? We are less open nowadays about our prejudices.

If it was right for this woman to challenge Jesus, surely it is still permissible for those outside the church's definition of itself to challenge its boundaries and structures and hierarchy. Even dogs eat the crumbs.

In this story, the issue is not rights. The woman does not
question Jesus' implication that, compared with Jews, she is a dog.
Today, it might be more likely that people would cry in rage: "I am
not a dog, but just as human as you." Or else take the animal rights
position that dogs count as much as people do. Neither of these
happens in the story. The focus is not on rights but on need.

When we are in need, can we get past others' claims about their
rights and our lack of rights? When others are in need, can we
forget our rights and respond to the need? If Jesus could learn from
a foreign woman, who is incapable of being a source of learning for
us?

Martha and Mary

Read: Luke 10:38-42
The Story. Jesus is visiting Martha and Mary at their home in
Bethany. While Martha prepares the meal, Mary sits at Jesus' feet
listening to him. Martha asks Jesus to command Mary to help.
Jesus responds, "Martha, Martha; you are worried and troubled
about may things but one thing is needful. Mary has chosen that
part, and it will not be taken away from her."

Analysis. Martha and Mary of Bethany appear together in the
gospels of both Luke and John. They are presented as sisters; Luke
adds a brother, Lazarus.

The story omits a great deal, and interpretations vary widely
depending on how these omissions are filled. Is the story about
different kinds of women's work, in general or in the church? Is it
about different kinds of ministry? Is it about speaking and silence?
How do Martha and Mary respond to Jesus' words? Does it make a
difference in their relationship or in their future behavior?

This story can be read as a legitimation of Mary and her behavior over Martha and hers. Such a reading may be appealing to
women in non-traditional roles, especially religious professionals.
Here is a text for us: Jesus himself legitimates a woman's choice to
ignore household work and spend her time on the words of Jesus.
Like Mary, we want to think, we have chosen the "one thing" that
is needed.

Yet Jesus' rebuke of Martha may be related less to the kind of work she is doing than to her being worried and distracted and imposing her worries on Mary. If that is true, we who are religious professionals must admit that we are just as likely to play Martha as those whose work is centered in the household.

In the story from Mary's point of view, the problem is not which kind of work is more important, but Martha's insistence on taking Mary away from her own setting. In such a reading, Jesus' rebuke to Martha can function as a call for every woman—working at home, in the church, or in another place—to respect her sisters' callings rather than insisting that hers is the only legitimate one.

From Martha's point of view the problem is too much work and not enough hands. Martha's problem is not resolved in the text. While Mary's choice is honored, Martha's overwork is not relieved. She is left with all the work she had before, but with the additional burden of Jesus' rebuke.

The story can be read in reference to the early Palestinian church, in which Mary and Martha were a pair of church leaders with distinct roles. Martha (the *diakonos* or deacon) was involved in the ministry of the table, and Mary (the *adelphe* or sister) in the ministry of the word.[5] In this reading, the tradition has Jesus affirming the ministry of the word, either generally or particularly, as an appropriate ministry for a woman.

Some interpreters suspicious of Luke's attitude toward women suggest that the story is an attempt to keep women quiet and submissive.[6] Mary is not teaching, after all, or even asking questions, but sitting quietly at Jesus' feet. Martha is the one who speaks, and she is immediately rebuked by Jesus. In such a reading, Luke gives Mary's role prominence to show that women are welcome in the Christian community, but he silences Martha to discourage women's active involvement, especially in leadership roles.

Reading from Below. What about Martha? I find myself disappointed in Jesus as Luke presents him here. Why didn't he ease Martha's burden? He could have said, "Martha, sit down and relax with us. I'd rather talk with the two of you than have a fancy meal. Let's eat cheese and olives tonight, and leave the fancy dinner for another time." Luke's Jesus says none of these things. 'The least' today may be those women whose work is taken for granted and who cannot call on their sisters for support and assistance.

What about Mary? What do you suppose happens after the end of the story? Does Jesus' teaching enable her to speak or keep her quiet? 'The least' may be those who hear the Gospel's call but always with a Luke in the background hinting that, although listening is fine, speaking is dangerous.

What about those of us who identify with Mary and then suppose it is all right for us to become worried and distracted in service of the word? It is just as destructive to get "Martha'd out" on Mary work. When one's distractions involve service to Jesus and the word, how is one appropriately called to Mary behavior?

It is impossible for me to read the story as it stands from the point of view of both Martha and Mary. Jesus legitimates Mary's choice but does nothing to alleviate Martha's burden: Mary wins and Martha loses. When I enter into the story from Mary's point of view, I am vindicated—but I have lost a sister. When I enter into it from Martha's point of view, I am frustrated—and I have lost a sister. The story presents a conflict between two women, two sisters, and ends with no hint of resolution.

I would like to blame the keepers of the tradition for telling stories that pit one woman and one ministry against another. Perhaps for this story that blame would be justified. John too tells of Martha and Mary, with no hint of conflict between them (John 11:1-12:8). But I am afraid that even if the shape of this specific story is the fault of patriarchal storytellers, there are plenty of situations in which women pit themselves against one another into win-lose situations.

When I read this story from below, I grieve. I would like to imagine a situation in which sisters act sisterly, each woman's work is affirmed, and they invoke the presence and authority of Jesus as Lord not to choose between them but to cement their sisterhood.

The Woman Who Anoints Jesus

Read: Mark 14:1-9
The Story. Two days before the Passover, while the religious authorities are looking for a way to arrest Jesus, he takes a meal at the house of Simon, a leper. A woman comes with an alabaster jar of expensive ointment, or nard, breaks open the jar, and pours the ointment on Jesus' head.

Some of those present object to wasting the ointment instead of selling it and spending the proceeds on the poor. Jesus, however, approves of her action: "Let her alone; why do you trouble her? She has performed a good service for me. For you always have the poor with you, and you can show kindness to them whenever you wish; but you will not always have me. She has done what she could; she has anointed my body beforehand for its burial. Truly I tell you, wherever the good news is proclaimed in the whole world, what she has done will be told in remembrance of her."

Analysis. This story is also told in Matt. 26:6-13. Similar stories appear in Luke 7:36-50 and John 12:1-8. In both Luke's and John's stories, Jesus' feet are anointed rather than his head. Luke presents the woman as a sinner, and the story becomes a challenge to Jesus' status as a prophet and an opportunity for teaching about forgiveness and response. As John tells it, the anointing takes place at the house of Martha of Bethany, and Mary does the anointing.

In all the versions except Luke's, this story takes place during the last week of Jesus' life. John makes Judas Iscariot the one who objects to the "waste" of money that could be spent on the poor. Although Matthew and Mark do not, they do pick up the theme by following this story immediately with a report of Judas going to the religious leaders and offering to betray Jesus.

The ointment itself and the alabaster bottle are expensive items. The bottle can be used only once because the oil is sealed in it. It must be broken to be used.

Elisabeth Schüssler Fiorenza reconstructs the earliest tradition as close to Mark's story. She points out that, in the biblical tradition, it is prophets who perform anointings, ordinarily of kings. Thus the woman is engaged in a prophetic action by which she proclaims Jesus as the Messiah (which literally means "anointed one"). Fiorenza also points out the irony in Jesus' statement that the story will continue to be told "in memory of her," because the tradition has not even remembered the woman's name.[7]

Reading from Below. Fiorenza's interpretation is an example of "reading from below" as a woman. The story also provides an opportunity for the poor to "read from below." What does it mean for Jesus to say, "For you always have the poor with you"? Is he accepting or even approving the existence of poverty? Is the story used properly when it is used to urge spending money on displays of extravagance rather than on social needs?

A conversation in *Voices from the Margins* records a conversation about this story in a Nicaraguan base community where today's poor, people who might have been the beneficiaries of the money spent instead on ointment, struggle with these questions.[8]

Participants in the conversation offer various possibilities. One suggests that the time of the story—the time just before Jesus' death—was the time for expensive ointment. But now, when Jesus is no longer physically with us, is the time for reaching out to the poor. Some struggle with "you always have the poor." Surely this is not an excuse to avoid struggling for change. Several identify Jesus with the poor: "When she offered it to Jesus, she was giving it, in his person, to all the poor."[9] "What she had present was Jesus, his person; now we have him present but in the person of the poor."[10] "So that we do it now, not to him anymore, but to the poor. Or to him in the person of the poor."[11]

The last exchange is poignant in its uniting of the woman's gift of ointment and Jesus' gift of himself:

Olivia: And people like us who don't have perfumes or luxurious things to give because we're poor?

Felipe: We can give other valuable things that we have.

Laureano: We can offer our lives as Jesus did. Then it'll be also for us, that perfume that the woman poured on Jesus.[12]

Mary Magdalene

Read: John 20:1-18

The Story. It is early, the first day of the week after Jesus' crucifixion. Mary Magdalene comes to the tomb. Seeing that the stone is gone, runs to tell Peter and the beloved disciple, "They have taken the Lord out of the tomb, and we do not know where they have laid him." The two men hurry to the tomb. The beloved disciple looks in and sees the wrappings. Peter follows, enters the tomb, and sees the wrappings. The other enters too and believes. Then the narrator adds: "For as yet they did not understand the scripture, that he must rise from the dead." The disciples return home.

Mary stands weeping, bends to look into the tomb, and sees two angels, who then ask her why she is weeping. "They have taken away my Lord, and I do not know where they have laid him." Then she turns and sees Jesus, but mistakes him for the gardener. He asks, "Woman, why are you weeping? Whom are you looking for?" She says, "Sir, if you have carried him away, tell me where you have laid him, and I will take him away." Jesus says, "Mary," and she responds, "My rabbi!" He tells her not to hold him, "because I have not yet ascended to the Father. But go to my brothers and say to them, 'I am ascending.'" Mary goes and tells the disciples.

Analysis. Mary Magdalene is the only person listed in all four gospels as being at the tomb on Easter morning. In both this text and Matt. 28:1-10 she is presented as the first witness to the risen Jesus—alone here and in Matthew with another Mary.

The text combines two traditions about Mary—that she was present at the discovery of the empty tomb and that she was a witness to the resurrection.[13] Between the two comes the visit by Peter and the beloved disciple, who are presented here as the first to actually look into the tomb and see that it is empty. No angel appears to the two male disciples to interpret the meaning of the empty tomb, but the beloved disciple believes.

The closing scene, in which Mary encounters first two angels and then the risen Jesus, may combine two separate traditions about Mary's experiences at the tomb. The appearance of the angels is unusual, first because Mary is not afraid, and second because here, unlike in the other gospel accounts, the angels do not proclaim the resurrection to her.[14]

The rest of the story echoes themes already expressed in John. Recognition when addressed by name recalls John 10:3-4, and the theme of Jesus' ascent or return to God "dominates references to the crucifixion in the Johannine discourses."[15] There is no promise to appear to the other disciples (as there is in the other gospels), although additional appearances do take place in John.

We do not know much about Mary Magdalene. She was in the band of disciples who followed Jesus (Luke 8:2), and seven demons were cast out of her (Luke 8:2; Mark 16:9). Other than that, she appears only in the death and resurrection narratives. Yet when women disciples are mentioned, her name always appears at the head of the list.

Although popular tradition understands her to be a prostitute, there is no biblical tradition behind this. Why do people read her as a prostitute when she is not presented that way in the Bible? Perhaps the only 'demonic' behavior that patriarchal cultures can imagine of women is sexual. It also appears that stereotypes of women in the Christian tradition have been split between the two Marys, Magdalene and Jesus' mother. Because the mother of Jesus is ascribed both the virgin and mother images, the only stereotype that is left for Magdalene is sexual availability.

Reading from Below. This story shows Jesus choosing one of "the least." Because Mary is a former sufferer from demonic possession, her word is likely to be even less credible than that of a typical woman—and no woman's testimony is legally valid. Although a careful reading of the Gospels shows that she is a leader among the disciples, her name is not among the twelve.

Mary sinks even lower in the church's tradition, which understands her to be a prostitute. In addition, she is a major figure in Christian Gnostic writings, and because gnosticism is rejected as heresy, Mary becomes suspect as well. We might wonder about this combination of factors, Mary as both prostitute and Gnostic hero. Gnosticism is known for making a dualizing distinction between the spiritual and the physical. Why would Gnostics give particular honor to a woman with a reputation for sexually free behavior? Might the traditional sexual understanding of Mary be anti-gnostic propaganda?

For Mary, to be 'the least' means to be a forgotten disciple. The dominant tradition has forgotten whether she was present at the last supper. It does not record her questions and comments when Jesus taught. The tradition is unable, however, to erase her presence at the cross and resurrection.

Who are the Magdalenes today? Who are the ones who know Jesus, who are always present but rarely noticed at church events? Who are the women and men who witness to the risen Christ but whose proclamations are not acclaimed until 'credible witnesses' repeat them? Who are the women and men whose illnesses are interpreted as sins?

How might these Magdalenes experience this story? How would they feel, hearing Jesus choose them as witnesses to the Resurrection, yet learning that the tradition will not remember their roles precisely? What would it mean to know that their illnesses will be remembered as sins?

Women in Parables

Women in parables that Jesus tells, more clearly than women in narratives about Jesus, are entirely fictional characters. As such, they reveal different aspects of his attitudes. The narratives tell us how the tradition remembers Jesus relating to women; the parables tell us how the tradition remembers Jesus imaging women. Both are valid concerns in learning how the tradition recalls Jesus' relationships with women.

The Woman Baking Bread
Read: Matthew 13:33
The Story. The kingdom of heaven is like a woman baking bread. She kneads a little yeast into a bushel of flour, and the yeast leavens the whole dough.

Analysis. This parable is best read in conjunction with the preceding one, in which a man plants a mustard seed. Both are parables in which something small has a large effect. (This is an unusual positive image of leaven: more often, leaven is imaged as contaminant. See, for example, Matt. 16:6,12; 1 Cor. 5:6-8; Gal. 5:9.)

The parable shows, on the one hand, an acceptance of women's traditional work. On the other hand, in conjunction with the parable of the mustard seed, it reinforces stereotypes of men working outdoors and women working in. This parable, then, both reinforces ideas about a woman's place and honors that place by making it an image for the kingdom of God.

The Woman and the Lost Coin
Read: Luke 15:8-10
The Story. The woman in this parable owns ten coins but has lost one. Rather than satisfying herself with the nine that she can find, she cleans her house in search of the tenth coin until she finds it. Then she rejoices with her friends and neighbors. The application is explicit: "So there is much rejoicing in heaven over one sinner who repents."

Analysis. The woman owns property in her own right. There is no mention of a connection with or dependence on a man. After she finds the coin, the woman calls her neighbors and friends (not a husband, son, or father) to celebrate. The parable does not make clear the reason for the woman's concerns. It could be either financial need of all ten coins or simply a desire to find and keep what is hers.

Because this parable is framed as a likeness to the reign of God, the woman is loosely figured as an image of God. This element is not stressed, but it demonstrates that it is not anathema to Jesus and the early church to imagine a woman as a way of representing God, however soft-focus the representation may be. Nor does Jesus hesitate to find an image of God in everyday domestic work. The woman does not commission children or servants to do the housecleaning; she sweeps the house herself.

The Wise and Foolish Bridesmaids
Read: Matthew 25:1–13

The Story. Bridesmaids are waiting for the bridegroom, who is late in arriving at the wedding celebration.[16] The young women all fall asleep and do not awaken until the groom arrives. The foolish bridesmaids discover that they have run out of oil, and the wise ones refuse to share: if they were to give up part of their oil, there would not be enough for anyone. The foolish ones run out to buy more oil. They arrive at the celebration too late and remain outside.

Analysis. Not enough is known about marriage rituals in New Testament times for us to be able to understand the customs behind this parable very well. Yet the affirmation remains: waiting for the reign of God is like being a young unmarried woman, wise or foolish.

The difference between the two groups is presented as the difference between wisdom and folly. Some planned ahead and brought extra oil; others did not. There is no hint of social class here. It does not appear that some bridesmaids could afford more oil than others. As unmarried women (girls, we would think of them, probably pre-menstrual), the bridesmaids are among 'the least' in terms of social power in their society.

The lack of concern for the foolish on the part of the wise may be disconcerting. This parable fits into two strains of Jesus' teaching. First, it is a call to be prepared for the manifestation of the reign of God. Second, it is a call to singleminded focus on the reign of God to such an extent that human relationships become irrelevant.

The Persistent Widow
Read: Luke 18:1–8

The Story. A widow is in need. She goes to a judge who is unjust and ignores her pleas. Yet the woman keeps after him until he finally grants her justice—not out of any sense of duty or righteousness but simply to get rid of her.

Analysis. The specifics of the woman's need are not described. Clearly she has no social power, yet she gets what she wants from a man with power, not through trickster means but simply by being persistent.

The framework of the parable suggests a correlation between God and an unjust judge. Although this correlation may be uncomfortable, it functions as "how much more" rather than as correspondence. That is, instead of suggesting that God is also unjust, it suggests that "if an unjust judge will listen to a woman with no social significance because of her persistence, how much more will God listen to you if you are persistent." The parable also allows the inference that sometimes God needs to be persuaded.

When the parable is read by itself, its interpretation is somewhat open. The possibilities are restricted, though, when one includes the parable's narrative context. Luke frames it with a moral: "They ought always to pray and not lose heart." The movement of the parable is similar to the movement in the narrative of Jesus and the Canaanite woman (discussed earlier in this chapter), a story which is not present in Luke.

Reading Parables from Below

There is remarkable variety in Jesus' presentation of women in parables. One striking feature is that none of these women is presented in familial relationship to men. Sometimes (as with the woman baking bread) these relationships are simply irrelevant to the story. Sometimes (as with the persistent widow) it is important that the woman not have a man to argue her case and legitimate her claim. Even in the wedding parable, which includes a groom and ten women, the women are presented independently of their family relationships. Neither the bride nor the groom's mother is present.

At the same time, the women in these parables are in typical women's roles—baking bread, cleaning house, serving as attendants at a wedding, appealing to a more powerful man. This suggests that Jesus thinks of women as persons, not limiting his perception of them to their roles in relationships. He is able to show respect and personal concern for women in traditional feminine roles. He shows them making decisions and participating actively in their own lives.

For women who think of themselves as powerless victims, these parables show a glimpse of a world in which women with roles much like their own are able to make wise or foolish decisions (how much oil to take to the wedding), make a big difference through a small action (kneading yeast into a loaf of bread), recover from mistakes (find the lost coin), take action against unjust social structures (persistent widow), and even symbolize the reign of God and (however loosely) God's own self.

In addition, because these parables are presumably presented to mixed audiences (men as well as women), they give men the opportunity to identify with women and women's roles and to see the potential for effective action within traditional women's roles.

Was Jesus a Feminist?

The combination of narratives about Jesus and parables of Jesus show him relating to and imagining women in ways unusual in his society. He sees women, within or outside of traditional roles, as individuals who make choices and effect change. This may tempt us to call him a feminist.

Nevertheless, the feminist label is an anachronism. Clearly Jesus would not have thought about sex and gender roles in the same way we do. He was a first-century man and did not perceive the issues in a twentieth-century framework. Still, it may be tempting to think of him as somehow anticipating feminism. If so, it is important that in our concern to show esteem for Jesus we not denigrate the surrounding culture. Sometimes Christian feminists make it

sound as though women are entirely invisible or oppressed within
Judaism until Jesus comes in and, in a total break with his culture,
relates to them perfectly. In an analysis of Christian feminism in
relation to Judaism, Judith Plaskow urges recognition that Jesus was
a first-century Jew. If his behavior toward women was more positive
than that of than most people in his culture, he represents a
possibility within the Judaism of his time and not a total break with
it.[17]

There is another danger in the 'Jesus as feminist' claim. Sometimes Christian feminists so connect their feminism with Jesus'
behavior toward women that it appears as if feminism is possible
only in relation to him. There are many Jewish feminists today. It is
important to recognize that Christianity does not provide the only
religious framework in which feminism is possible in the biblical
heritage. If feminism is possible for you because of Jesus, fine. But
if you claim that he is the only possibility for feminism in biblically
based religions, you deny Jewish feminists the right to exist.

The claim that Jesus represents a possibility within first-century
Judaism and not a total break with it is based not only on theory.
Both textual and historical studies make it clear that there were
different tendencies during this period, both within Judaism and in
the surrounding culture. Women are celebrated in story and were
strong characters within some Jewish communities of Jesus' times.
While we may emphasize Jesus as remarkable within his heritage
and context, it is important not to deny that he also reflects that
heritage and context.

Chapter Five

Women in the Garden
Interpreting the Tradition

There are two major biblical texts involving women and gardens—the story of Eden and the Song of Songs (or Song of Solomon). These two may be interpreted in counterpoint to one another. Combined, the two texts can provide balance for one another. And yet, only one of them, the Eden story, has functioned in Western tradition to shape basic beliefs about women. In this chapter we will examine and question the interpretive tradition of these two texts and look at recent attempts to reinterpret the tradition itself.

Losing the Garden

Eve is basic to Western understandings of women and particularly women's roles in relation to men. It is very difficult for women in our culture to come to terms with their roles in society and the church without confronting the Eve story and the history of its use. So the first half of this chapter is largely about Eve.

It is widely accepted that there are two tellings of creation in the early chapters of Genesis. The first creation account, while distinct from the Eden story, provides the narrative context for its development. In addition, there are creation texts elsewhere in the Bible that suggest a different story as their background.[1] The Genesis accounts are emphasized here both because of the prominence of Eve and because their position at the beginning of the canonical books of the Bible makes them the texts we think of when we begin to consider creation.

The Priestly Creation Text

Read: Genesis 1:1-2:4a

This is a stately text, carefully ordered. In fact, its concern is with order. Creation is depicted not only as production but also as classification. In the act of creating, God makes a series of distinctions and, within them, correspondences. The text falls into three sections. In section one, the first through third days, God distinguishes light from darkness, sky from water, and dry land from sea. In section two, the fourth through sixth days, God creates the creatures corresponding to these newly distinguished habitats—sky creatures (sun, moon, and stars) on day four, air and water creatures on day five, and earth creatures on day six. The third, culminating section is the seventh day, the day of rest, the Sabbath.

This is a monotheizing text in which the sea and sun are seen not as deities competing for power with Israel's God, but as creations of the one God. Even the cycles of the newly created natural world are superseded by the seven-day cycle which culminates in the weekly Sabbath.[2]

Sabbath, though, is not the last work of creation. Rather, it is the sign that the work has been completed. Human beings, in the image of God, male and female, are the last of the creatures, prelude to the divine rest on the Sabbath:

> Then God said: "Let us make humankind in our image, according to our likeness; and let them have dominion over the fish of the sea, and over the birds of the air, and over the cattle, and over all the wild animals of the earth, and over every creeping thing that creeps upon the earth."
> So God created humankind in his image,
> in the image of God he created them;
> male and female he created them.
> God blessed them, and God said to them, "Be fruitful and multiply, and fill the earth and subdue it; and have dominion over the fish of the sea and over the birds of the air and over every living thing that moves upon the earth." God said, "See, I have given you every plant yielding seed that is upon the face of all the earth, and every tree with seed in its fruit; you shall have them for food." (Gen. 1:26-29)

An obvious question is, Why does God speak in the plural? God speaks of *our* image and *our* likeness. The traditional Christian answer to this question has been that this is an early reference to the Trinity. But this makes sense only within communities that accept the Trinity. It cannot be what the text meant for the community in which it was first used, because the doctrine of the Trinity had not yet been developed. For that community, the plural more likely reflected the idea of a divine council, a group of heavenly beings with Yahweh at their head.

The Hebrew word translated as "humankind" is 'adam, a word that can mean people in general or a specific human being. It is not the word that is normally used to specify a male individual. Should any doubt remain, the text goes on to specify "male and female."

In its original setting, the text would not have suggested equality of women and men in social power or social function. There is no evidence that these were issues for ancient Israelite society, and thus it is unlikely that Israelites would have composed and told these stories to reflect on issues of gender equality. Yet the text does imply an affirmation of human sexual difference as part of the divine choice in creation, male and female as the image of God, and male and female as included in the "very good" spoken over all creation in Gen. 1:31.

The Eden Story

Read: Genesis 2:4b–3:24

The Shape of the Story. As we move from the first to the second account of creation, the images of God and God's work change. God is no longer described as a stately, magisterial speaker, as in the priestly story, but rather as an active worker. We might see hints of Yahweh as potter in 2:7, as farmer in 2:8, and as surgeon and architect in 2:21-22. Yahweh forms an earthling from clay, plants a garden, and brings animals to the earthling for naming. Among these animals, no suitable partner[3] for the earthling is found. So God becomes a surgeon, anesthetizing the earthling to remove a rib, and then an architect, building a new creature, woman, out of that rib. Upon regaining consciousness, the earthling exclaims:

> This at last is bone of my bones
> and flesh of my flesh;

this one shall be called Woman,
for out of Man this one was taken. (Gen. 2:23)

There is a great deal of debate about the importance of these verses. Was the original earthling male or ungendered? That is, in the surgical-architectural process, was a female created from a male, or were male and female created from a sexually undifferentiated being? If the former is the case, does God's creating woman from man indicate subordination (as if she were an afterthought), or superiority (paralleling the creation of humans in Genesis 1)? Is "this one shall be called Woman" a naming formula, indicating that the namer has authority over the one who is named, or does naming occur only at the end of the events of chapter 3?[4] It seems to me that the text is spare enough to be open to differing interpretations. Although there is no clear indication of male superiority in the text, neither is there a clear claim of equality. The difference between the two humans is presented but not evaluated.

The story continues in chapter 3. There is in the garden a serpent, and the serpent invites the woman to eat from the tree Yahweh has forbidden. The woman does. She gives some of the fruit to the man who is "with her,"[5] and he eats. Yahweh arrives, and the humans hide. When Yahweh questions the man, he blames the woman; the woman then blames the serpent. Yahweh then informs all three of the consequences of their actions.

The consequences of the serpent's actions are that it is cursed—from now on it will crawl on its belly and eat dirt—and humans and snakes will hate each other, but humans will have greater power.[6]

The consequences of the woman's actions are that childbirth will be painful and difficult, and she will desire a man who will relate to her by dominating her.

The consequences of the man's actions are that the ground will be cursed and work will be difficult and sweaty. He will farm for a living, and the ground will fight him until he dies and returns to it.

The man then names the woman Eve, which is similar to the Hebrew word for "life." Yahweh clothes the two humans and sends them out of the garden.

Eve's Role. Is the woman presented in the story as a strong, capable actor or as a weak, inept sinner? Several elements of the story are significant for the interpretation of her role:

1. It is before the "surgery" on the earthling, before the distinct existence of the woman, that Yahweh gives the command, "You may freely eat of every tree of the garden; but of the tree of the knowledge of good and evil you shall not eat, for in the day that you eat of it you shall die" (Gen. 2:16–17). If one understands the original earthling in continuity with the man and not the woman, this means that her knowledge depends on what he has told her.

2. The woman misquotes the divine command to include not only eating from the tree but also touching it. The text does not say whether she lies, remembers wrong, or was misinformed.

3. As we have noted, the man is apparently with the woman throughout her conversation with the snake.

4. In the scene with the serpent, the man is not reported as speaking, either to the serpent or to the woman, until Yahweh appears. The man and woman never speak directly to each other.

All of these elements have a bearing on Eve's role, but several of them create gaps in the text. The way an interpreter fills these gaps creates a direction for interpretation.

The Interpretive History of the Text. The tradition has judged Eve harshly. According to interpreters over the centuries, she sinned first; therefore, she is the one on whose account sin is part of human existence. Christian tradition has understood the Eden story as the Fall and blamed the Fall on Eve. The tradition has extended the behavior of the woman character in the Eden story to the behavior of all women: in her eating, all women ate. The consequences of her behavior have been understood as a curse expressing the divine will, a curse extended to apply to all women, so that God wants men to dominate women.

This is the kind of interpretation many of us grew up hearing. But the story did not always have this kind of paradigmatic power. Carol Meyers points out that the story is not quoted at all in the Hebrew Bible after the opening chapters of Genesis.[7] So at least we may conclude that the interpretation that is "traditional" for us did not function in that way for ancient Israel. In fact, it was only during the second temple period that the rejection of all women through Eve began.[8] The problem for Christian women is that it was during this very Greco-Roman period that the New

Testament documents were written, and one of them incorporates this negative reading of Eve:[9]

> I permit no woman to teach or to have authority over a man; she is to keep silent. For Adam was formed first, then Eve; and Adam was not deceived, but the woman was deceived and became a transgressor. (1 Tim. 2:12-14)

For Christians, not only the story but also a particular interpretive slant belongs to the canonical scriptures. In addition, because many Christians are more familiar with the New Testament than with the Old, some actually know this particular interpretation better than the story itself. People who grew up in English-language culture may also have confused the biblical story with Milton's version in *Paradise Lost*.

Rethinking Eden and Eve. In recent years, a number of studies of the Eden story have re-examined traditional interpretations. Among the most influential is Phyllis Trible's "A Love Story Gone Awry." According to this reading, the woman in the Eden story is presented as a strong, capable theologian, in contrast to the man, who is a passive follower. While the serpent is cursed directly and the man indirectly, only the woman is not cursed at all. The consequences of the woman's behavior are presented as punishment but not curses.

Carol Meyers reads the Eden story in the context of Israel's settlement period, during which she believes it originated. According to her, the text serves to explain the difficult circumstances of peasant life in the highlands during Israel's early history and to encourage the hard work and large families essential to survival during this subsistence period.[10]

How are we to read the sayings of Yahweh in Genesis 3:14-19? We might begin by asking why the Israelites might have told this story in the first place. My suspicion is that the text originates from observations about existence in the world. Snakes crawl on the ground. People and snakes make trouble for each other. Childbirth hurts, and women sometimes die giving birth. Women desire men, but the men are domineering. Farming is hard work but necessary for survival. Weeds and thistles spring up where farmers are trying to grow productive crops. People die and are buried, and in time the corpses disintegrate. Noticing these things, people told a story.

The story comes to terms with some difficult aspects of existence.

If this is a correct reconstruction (and it is a guess, open to question), then the consequences in Genesis 3:14-19 are not normative but descriptive. That is, they tell us not how life is supposed to be but how life happened to be experienced by the people who told and preserved this story.

What is especially interesting to me is that, of all the consequences described for the man's and woman's behavior, only one has usually been understood normatively, and that is the last of the woman's consequences. Very few people have supposed that because of the Eden story, it is wrong for men to engage in occupations other than farming. (Even Jesus wasn't a farmer.) Nor have people assumed that because men's work is supposed to make them sweat, they shouldn't work indoors or live in cold climates. And I have never heard anyone suggest that it is wrong to use herbicides because thistles and thorns grow by divine command.

Even with regard to the woman's consequences, most have not been taken as normative. As far as I know, no one suggests that because childbirth is supposed to be as painful and dangerous as possible, it is a sin to try to reduce the death rate in childbirth or to learn exercises to control pain. People who reject anesthetics and painkillers in childbirth generally do not do so on the theory that God has commanded pain in childbirth.

It is just the one consequence—"your man . . . will dominate you—that has been taken as normative.[11] Out of all the consequences in these verses, this is the one about which people have said, "Yes, that's the way it should be, the way God wants it, and we are going to do our best to fulfill God's will."

What if all the consequences described for the woman and the man were descriptive instead of normative? What if all of them reflected a recognition that something had gone wrong with the creation, that its goodness had been distorted? What if all of them show not the will of God for creation but how human behavior can frustrate the will of God? Then men's domination of women would be an evil to be fought, just as the thistles that thwart productive farming and the death of women in childbirth are.

Adam and Eve can be interpreted as original humankind, the first human beings, or as archetypes, symbolic of every human being. (Adam means "human being," and Eve means "life.") When one views them as primal, the decision to choose knowledge over obedience, to strive to be "like gods" has already been made, and we have no choice in the matter. But when one views them as archetypal, we all see ourselves in them: as they chose, so we choose. And when we have chosen, we pay the consequences. The story is open to either reading. We live in a world of pain and toil and death because it has been that way from the beginning (we have no choice). And we suffer pain and alienation from our work and death because we ourselves insist on testing the boundaries of our circumstances (we have a choice).

The Relation of the Two Creation Texts. These two accounts of creation (the priestly text in Gen. 1:1–2:4a and the Eden story in 2:4b–3:31) are different in both style and function. Yet they are placed together at the beginning of Genesis, and the effect of that juxtaposition is that we understand the two in relation to each other. When we do this, we may perceive an irony between the "image of God" in 1:26 and the desire to "be like God" in 3:5. We may also understand Genesis 3 as a response to dissonance between the "very good" of 1:31 and human experience with all its difficulties. The "very good" is not undone; but the negative side of human life is allowed to come into the picture "from the beginning." Human life involves alienation from God, from our work, and from each other, but it also involves the affirmation that creation is "very good" and striving to recover as much of the goodness as possible.

The Song of Songs

Our second garden text, the Song of Songs (or Song of Solomon) is an idealization of a love relationship. It can be read as an undoing of what went wrong in Eden.[12] We cannot assume that it describes a typical love relationship in ancient Israel, but we can be sure that this is one way (not necessarily the only way) in which ancient Israelites might idealize love relationships. In other words, this kind of relationship is something that was hungered for in Israel.

Interpreters of the Song ask: Is it a song, a collection of songs, or a drama? There is not a critical consensus about either the unity or the genre of the text.[13] Apparently its ancestry includes more than one song, but refrain lines and repeated motifs provide a kind of unity to the final form.[14] Refrain lines include, "I adjure you, O daughters of Jerusalem . . . do not stir up or awaken love until it is ready" (Song of Sol. 2:7, 3:5, 8:4); "His left hand under my head/ and his right hand embracing me"[15] (Song of Sol. 2:6, 8:3), and "Who is this?" (Song of Sol. 3:6, 6:10, 8:5).[16] Themes include the garden, the vineyard, and seeking and finding. Motifs include lovesickness, invitations, and lilies. In addition there are several references to houses (the mother's house or the lover's house).

While the Song does not always come across as unified and coherent, neither is falling in love an entirely coherent and unified experience. The rapid shifts of scene and mood seem to me better to reflect the experience of love than do precisely balanced compositions such as the love sonnets of Western literature. Thus I choose to interpret the Song as a unity.

The authorship of the Song is unknown. Tradition ascribes it to Solomon because of the superscription, "The Song of Songs, which is Solomon's" (1:1). This could mean authorship by Solomon, but it could also be a dedication to Solomon, a claim that it was produced in the royal court of Solomon, or an awareness that it was the kind of text associated with Solomon (of whom it is said in 1 Kings 4:32 that he composed a thousand and five songs). Very few contemporary interpreters believe that Solomon was the author. There is no indication in the Song that Solomon is the speaker, and when he is mentioned (1:1, 5; 3:7, 9, 11; 8:11, 12) it is never in the first person.

Who then is the author? This is an intriguing question, but impossible to answer. Some interpreters suggest that the Song might have been written by a woman.[17] Given the amount of attention devoted to the woman character's experience and emotions, this text seems as likely as anything in the Bible to have been written by a woman. Yet it is also possible that the Song was written by a man, or by several authors, perhaps including both women and men.

This uncertainty raises an interesting problem for interpreters who want to understand the Song and what it says about ideals for male/female relationships in ancient Israel. It could be that we have here a woman's fantasies about the ideal male/female relationship or a man's fantasies about such a relationship. Or it could be that a woman is fantasizing the female character and a man the male character. It could be the other way around. The author's voice is not clear, and if we wish to use the Song to understand views of sexual love in ancient Israel, it does make a difference whose dreams we are hearing. Yet, if we are to interpret the Song at all, the question of authorship must be suspended. We cannot prove it one way or the other.

The characters in the Song include a woman and a man (some would say several women and several men), a chorus of Jerusalem women, the woman's brothers, and the city sentinels. Solomon appears in the distance. The woman's mother is also mentioned, but she is not actually present or quoted in the text.

The Story of the Song

The Song tells a story of yearning, of desire. It expresses love between a young woman and a young man whose relationship is somehow blocked because the woman's brothers object (1:6; 8:9). She cannot find the man (3:1–2; 5:6). The city sentinels beat her (5:7). Yet she dreams of the man (5:2, and perhaps 3:1) and roams the city streets looking for him. Her desire, when she finds him, is to take him to her mother's house (3:4, 8:2).

The man also speaks of his admiration and desire for the woman. Twice he invites her to come away (2:8–14; 4:8), but in general he is less active and less vocal than she.

There are also interludes that may express fulfilled desire (e.g., 2:3–4). Some passages are not clearly identified as either statements of what has happened or as wishes. Rather, they simply provide images. When the woman says, "his left hand under my head, his right embracing me,"[18] this may be a wish for what may happen, a description of what has happened, or an image that implies neither precisely but evokes the possibility.

The Poetry of the Song

Descriptive Motifs. Several times during the Song, one of the two speakers describes the other's body part by part, either head to foot or foot to head.[19] The man describes the woman in 4:1–7 and 7:1–7 and begins another such description in 6:4–7. The woman describes the man in 5:10–16. Feminists sometimes find a visual emphasis demeaning: to reduce a woman to a visual object is to refuse to deal with her as a person.[20] In the Song, however, the descriptive motifs do not appear to function to reduce the woman to an object. The motifs are used by both the man and the woman describing the other. In fact, the most visual and objectified passage occurs in the woman's description of the man:

> My beloved is all radiant and ruddy,
>> distinguished among ten thousand.
> His head is the finest gold;
>> his locks are wavy,
>> black as a raven.
> His eyes are like doves
>> beside springs of water,
> bathed in milk,
>> fitly set.
> His cheeks are like beds of spices,
>> yielding fragrance.
> His lips are lilies,
>> distilling liquid myrrh.
> *His arms are rounded gold,*
>> *set with jewels.*
> *His body is ivory work,*
>> *encrusted with sapphires.*
> *His legs are alabaster columns,*
>> *set upon bases of gold.*
> His appearance is like Lebanon,
>> choice as the cedars.
> His speech is most sweet,
>> and he is altogether desirable.
> This is my beloved and this is my friend,
>> O daughters of Jerusalem. (Song of Sol. 5:10–16)

Of all the descriptive motifs in the Song, this is the one that sounds the most objectified. The emphasized portion could be describing a statue. Most of its images are visual (exceptions include the fragrance of cheeks, myrrh of lips, and sweetness of speech). But this motif does not seem to reduce the beloved to an object. It moves from appearance to speech and ends in friendship.

The descriptive motifs in which the man describes the women are neither static nor exclusively visual. The most striking is this:

> How graceful are your feet in sandals,
>> O queenly maiden!

Your rounded thighs are like jewels,
 the work of a master hand.
Your navel is a rounded bowl
 that never lacks mixed wine.
Your belly is a heap of wheat,
 encircled with lilies.
Your two breasts are like two fawns,
 twins of a gazelle.
Your neck is like an ivory tower.
Your eyes are pools in Heshbon,
 by the gate of Bath-rabbim.
Your nose is like a tower of Lebanon,
 overlooking Damascus.
Your head crowns you like Carmel,
 and your flowing locks are like purple;
 a king is held captive in the tresses.
How fair and pleasant you are,
 O loved one, delectable maiden!
You are stately as a palm tree,
 and your breasts are like its clusters.
I say I will climb the palm tree
 and lay hold of its branches.
Oh, may your breasts be like clusters of the vine,
 and the scent of your breath like apples,
and your kisses like the best wine
 that goes down smoothly,
 gliding over lips and teeth. (Song of Sol. 7:1–9)

Unlike the previously described woman's song, this does not sound like the description of an object. The imagery begins in the visual but moves through all the senses. Clearly, it does not reduce the woman to an object. It feels almost as though the speaker were not entirely in control of the imagery, as though metaphors and similes were taking on a life of their own and running away.

This fluidity of imagery is especially noticeable in the italicized portion of the text. Having described the woman from feet to hair, the speaker summarizes the whole of her in the image of a palm tree but cannot stay in the realm of the general. Not only is her total form like a palm tree, but her breasts are its (date) clusters. Then the logic of the imagery moves from detached description to interaction. What does one do with a tree? Climb it, of course. By the time the speaker has climbed the tree, it is no longer a date palm but a grape vine combined with an apple tree. Then the woman is no longer an object on which the speaker acts but an agent in her own right, actively kissing the speaker with intoxicating kisses. If anyone loses power of action, it seems to be the male speaker, under the influence of the wine-kiss. In fact, he does seem to lose the power to act or at least to express his actions: the passage ends.

The imagery in this passage may seem bizarre to our modern, Western ears. Romantic imagery is often culturally specific, evocative rather than flatly descriptive. When we hear a description of lips as roses, for example, we know that we are not to think of thorns, but we don't know the cultural code for understanding "Your nose is like a tower of Lebanon," so we revert to the visual. This says something about the differences in associations from one culture to another but nothing about what is inherently odd. To read such a poem, we must suspend our culture's notions of what is legitimate imagery and enter into the mood of the text.[21]

Image Groups. Looking more generally at the images of the Song, we notice that there are groups of images more likely associated with one or the other character. One group contains rural, farming, and shepherding imagery. This image group is used of both characters but primarily of the man. Military images are used primarily of the woman, as is urban and architectural language. Wild animal imagery is associated with the man. Food and drink images are associated with both lovers but most often with the woman. Royal imagery is associated with both. Gardening and vine images pertain mostly to the woman. The lovers use sister and brother images for each other, but other family images are used exclusively for and by the woman, who refers to her mother and brothers but never to her father. There is no use of explicitly religious imagery or language, except perhaps one reference to God's name.[22] There are no references to children

There is also a great deal of sensory imagery in the Song—sight, smell, touch, sound, and taste. The sexual imagery is veiled in double entendre (for example, "He browses among the lilies" in 2:16, 6:3;[23] see also 7:2). It is allusive and evocative but not explicit.

Some of the images fit what we know of biblical love imagery, especially that of a garden or vineyard for the woman.[24] And some of it may make sense in our own culture: the fact that the woman speaks of family while the man does not mirrors our cultural notion that women are more attuned to relationships and intimacy than men are.

In other ways, however, the distribution of imagery seems strange, and this, I think, is particularly true of the association of battle and military images with the woman. At the very least, this suggests that the Israelites' social ideas about what is masculine and what is feminine may have been different from our own. These images may also evoke the sense of entering into a powerful situation that one cannot entirely control, the same idea evoked in our own culture by the expression "falling in love."

Although there is family imagery, there is no explicit marriage imagery, and this is also odd, especially if we have been reading the Song of Songs as a marriage poem or an allegory on the divine/human relationship. If it is a marriage song, it is surprising that there is no reference to a hope for children (we have already seen how important children are in Israelite culture) and no reference to specific mutual obligations (such as financial support or dowry). In fact, there is no discussion of rights and responsibilities at all except perhaps the mutual possession formula ("my beloved is mine and I am his"). Rather, the poem is about self-giving and desire.

From our cultural distance, it is difficult to know what to say about this lack. It is possible that the Song, although clearly about sexual love, is not really about marriage. If it is designed for marriage, the legal elements might be covered elsewhere. Or it could be that in an idealization of love, the poet chooses to ignore practical realities. Alternatively, the Song might encourage us to reconsider our own ideas about marriage as contract and enter more fully into the ideal of mutual self-giving and less into a discussion of rights and duties.

The Theology of the Song

As we have noted, there is at most one explicitly religious reference in the entire Song, and perhaps none. Yet I cannot read this as a purely secular poem. My reading is affected by the fact that the Song is part of the canon, which I understand as sacred Scripture. I find myself reading the Song with the idea that Yahweh approves. Whether the poet meant it that way or not, in its canonical context the Song functions as a very long commentary on the "very good" spoken over creation, especially spoken over the creation of humankind as male and female.

At the same time, it is important not to lose sight of the very human nature of the love in this Song. The Song takes place in an earthly setting, and the characters are human beings. In spite of efforts to read this as an Israelite version of a sacred marriage ritual,[25] there is no hint of gods and goddesses participating in the romance. If there is theology in the text, it is a theology of the goodness of creation (and situating sexuality within that goodness), not an elevation of sexuality to the divine.

The Purpose of the Song

Why would such a text be composed and preserved in ancient Israel? There are some who suppose that, in a patriarchal society, all erotic literature exists for men. The problem I find with this view as it applies to the Song of Songs is that this text does not appear to serve male interests in relation to sexuality. In particular, the Song does not support men's control of women's sexuality.[26] The brothers are seen as an obstacle to the relationship, but they are not able to prevent it. The city sentinels, too, are seen as attempting to control the woman, but they are unable to keep the relationship from continuing. While the text thus hints at male competition over property rights to a woman's body, in the end the woman still insists, "My vineyard, my very own, is for myself" (8:12). As we have seen, even the male lover's gaze at the woman does not fix her as an object.

It is possible to imagine the Song being used at weddings, but (as noted) it is surprising that a wedding song would not mention the usual expectations of marriage, especially children. It is also possible that the Song was composed as entertainment. The closest parallels to the Song in ancient Near Eastern literature are Egyptian love songs. One group of such songs gives them the label "pleasure of the heart," which may suggest diversion.[27] If so, such songs may have been sung as part of public celebrations on festivals. "To explain how the Song came to be regarded as part of the sacred literature of Israel, it may be enough to postulate that the Song, though not intrinsically religious, was sung as part of the entertainment and merrymaking at feasts and celebrations, which would naturally take place for the most part on holidays in the religious calendar."[28] It is also possible to imagine (but impossible to prove) that the Song may be a midrash or loose commentary on the Eden story.

Although later interpretations in both Judaism and Christianity present the Song as symbolic of the relationship between God and the people of God, this is not likely the original meaning. As Fox points out, "Equality is the essence of the relationship between the young lovers in the Song, and this an hardly have been intended as a model for God's relation to Israel."[29]

Jewish and Christian Use of the Song

What are we to do with such a Song in our Bible? Judeo-Christian tradition offers two possibilities: we may interpret it symbolically (ignore the specific, natural references to sexual love between a woman and a man) or ignore it (as do all standard weekly lectionaries). Traditional interpretations of the Song in Judaism and Christianity have understood it as an image of the relationship between the human and the divine. Within Judaism, it has been primarily interpreted in terms of the relationship between God and Israel. In Christianity it has more often been understood to express the relationship between Christ and the church. In both types of interpretation, the reader identifies with the woman of the Song.

Among both Jewish and Christian mystics, it is sometimes possible to partially reverse this identification. Some Jewish interpreters have identified with the male lover and interpreted the female lover as the Shekinah (or Presence) of God, personified as a woman.[30] Within Sephardic (Eastern) Judaism, the entire Song is read every Sabbath, thus suggesting a symbolic identification of the woman in the Song with the Sabbath, personified as bride.

There is nothing wrong with romance or marriage as an image for the divine-human relationship, and indeed it is valuable to have a positive version of this image,[31] but I am disappointed, not that these interpretations exist, but that for so long they blocked the natural understanding of the Song as an expression of human love. Our own culture seems to be split in its attitude toward sex. In some parts of the culture, expressions of sexuality are not only open but suggest that the only restraint is self-interest (such as fear of sexually transmitted diseases). Others (including much of the church) do not mention sex except obliquely or negatively. The Song can lead us to reclaim the holiness of a sexuality that is neither promiscuous nor ashamed. This is not to suggest that sexuality is incapable of abuse or that desire always leads to good. Yet I believe that an honest appreciation of the pleasure and promise of sexuality in a canonical context is a healthy way to embark on young people's sexual education. The Song can also give canonical permission for shy couples to speak openly about sex and sexual pleasure in a context not of mutual demands but of mutual invitation and self-giving. When relationships become bogged down with the mundane details of life—mortgages and braces and who is responsible for being home when the plumber comes—it may be time to reawaken to the garden of sensual delight.

The Two Gardens: Genesis and the Song

I have already mentioned that it is possible to read the Song as a commentary on the "very good" spoken over creation of male and female. It is also possible to read it, as Phyllis Trible does, as a vision of the undoing of the mishap in Eden.[32] It is impossible to determine whether the text is consciously intended to be contrasted with the Eden story, but there is a real contrast in themes and an overlap in language. Life includes both sad recognitions (childbirth is painful and dangerous; men dominate women) and joyful possibilities (loving desire can be as strong as death). Thematically, the Eden story moves from "very good" to a sense of distorted relationships, whereas the Song is a reclaiming of the "very good." In terms of language, the most striking is the reversal of "your desire shall be for your man" (Gen. 3:16, my translation) to "his desire is for me" (Song of Sol. 7:10). Desire, the Eden story acknowledges, can provide an occasion for domination, but the Song is a reminder that it can also be offered freely.

Chapter Six

Gender and God
Constructive Biblical Theology

The goal of this chapter is to 'do theology'—that is, to talk about God. The question we will address is: How should biblical language and images about God shape the use of gender language in our own ways of thinking and talking about God? Resources for this reflection include the Bible, gender studies, language studies, and an awareness of our own cultural situation. Our goal is to reflect on responsible ways of speaking about God today.

In the course of this chapter, I will of course tell you how I fit these pieces together. Yet the purpose of this chapter is not to persuade you to agree with me, but to help you to think about some of the issues involved in deciding how you yourself will talk about and image God.

Preliminary Issues

The "Problem" of Truth

This chapter is more complicated for me than it would be for many writers. The problem is that I believe in God and that, moreover, I identify the God I worship with the God revealed in the Bible. The question of the identity of the God of the Bible is not, for me, merely a question of what the ancient Israelites and early Christians (including biblical authors) believed. Rather, it is a question of truth: Who is this God, really?

For many people nowadays, it is somewhat embarrassing to speak of truth. In our time, it is more fashionable to acknowledge that all things are relative. What looks true to me is affected by who I am and where and when I live. I am acknowledging that when I say, "I believe." I am not trying to insist that you believe the same thing. But for me it is important to talk about God from the perspective of faith today, not only from the perspective of historical reconstruction.

This chapter contains a combination of historical information and theological discussion. Although I try to distinguish my beliefs from the background information that shapes those beliefs, it is inevitable that those beliefs also shape the way I receive and interpret the background information.

Unity and Diversity in Biblical Theology

It is clear that biblical writers did not all have the same understanding of God. It is equally clear that they lived in societies in which people had widely differing religious beliefs and practices. We might find it helpful to return to a distinction made in chapter one among popular religion, official religion, and canonical religion.

Canonical religion—that is, religion as urged by the editors of the biblical text—is monotheistic Yahwism without any images. There is not much ritual described in canonical texts, although there are references to rituals. The books of the Hebrew Bible are edited to promote the idea that the Jerusalem temple is the only place where Yahweh is willing to be worshiped.

Canonical religion contains only vague memories of women's roles in the cult and specific women's rituals. Work to recover these on the basis of textual hints and archaeological finds is now taking place.

In the New Testament, canonical religion is concerned with understanding and proclaiming the significance of Jesus as Messiah, his relationship to God, and the sense of his continued presence in the believing community. New Testament canonical religion is careful to interpret itself in the context of the Old Testament.

Official religion in the Hebrew Bible was that urged by the state and practiced at officially sanctioned shrines. It included forms of worship that are not acceptable within canonical religion. There were multiple shrines for Yahweh, although the Bible is edited to urge worship only at the Jerusalem temple. Some scholars believe that the goddess Asherah was worshiped as Yahweh's consort.[1] There were probably significant differences between the official religions of the northern and southern kingdoms. Because the northern kingdom fell first, its traditions are preserved only as filtered through the south. Yet refugees from the north clearly left their mark on southern traditions.

Because the early church was not identified with a state, it is more difficult to speak of official religion. In the later books of the New Testament (such as 1 and 2 Timothy), however, we begin to see more centralized leadership and concern with uniformity within the church itself. The church as institution is developing its own official religion.

Popular religion is what the common people actually thought and did. Clearly, at various periods of Israelite history, popular religion included the worship of deities other than Yahweh, including Baal (1 Kings 19) and the "Queen of heaven" (Jer. 7:18, 44:17-25).

In the New Testament, popular religion includes a variety of beliefs and practices. The letters of Paul often include discussions of issues in which the popular religion of a given congregation is at odds with Paul's claims for official religion. The New Testament reflects a period of sorting out which elements of popular religion will be acceptable within official religion.

Polytheism, Monolatry, Monotheism, and Dualism

Polytheism means belief in many gods, while monotheism means belief in only one. Monolatry means the *worship* of only one god, although one may believe that other gods exist.

The cultures surrounding the Israelites were polytheistic. In these cultures, different divine characteristics and functions were ascribed to different deities, represented as male or female and often depicted in human, animal, or other images. An individual, family, or political unit might offer special devotion to one of these deities, but that would not mean denying the existence or power of others.

The worship of many gods is clearly rejected throughout the Bible, although it is obvious that in their popular religion, many Israelites did worship gods other than Yahweh, and this may also have been true in official religion. James Sanders has a helpful way of speaking about this distinction between what the Israelites believed and what the Bible suggests. He says that although the Israelites were not historically a monotheizing people, the Bible is a monotheizing literature.[2] It is not so easy, though, to determine what lies *behind* biblical texts. When is the unspoken background monotheisim and when is it monolatry? For example, the commandment "You shall have no other gods before me" (Exod. 20:3; Deut. 5:7) does not explicitly deny the existence of other deities.[3]

During the exile, if not before, there were true monotheists among the Israelites in Babylon. (This is clear from Isaiah 44:9-20, a satire on the worship of idols which demonstrates that the author does not understand how people who use images in worship think about them.) It is not so clear, though, whether such figures as Moses and Elijah objected to the worship of deities other than Yahweh because they believed that Yahweh was the only God or because they believed that worshiping other gods, even if they existed, meant being unfaithful to Yahweh.

Sometimes one hears people (feminist or anti-feminist) speaking as if the demise of polytheism, especially goddess-oriented polytheism, were the source of patriarchy. It can sound as if there were a natural progression from worship of a pantheon headed by a goddess to worship of a pantheon with a high male god to the elimination of all the other gods. This process of eliminating all divine power but that of the high male god is understood to parallel a process of eliminating all social power but that of the high male caste. According to this scenario, a strong part of the agenda of monotheism (often described as *male* monotheism) is to eliminate the possibility of worshiping a goddess, which is extended to even thinking of God in female terms, so that eventually the idea of deity is equated with the idea of the masculine.

I am not persuaded by this argument, particularly as it relates to the development of Yahwistic monotheism. From the time Yahwism first appears, it seems to be understood as a religion of liberation for the underclass. This is clear from the exodus from Egypt, the founding event in Yahwistic religion, which is described in Israelite memory as a liberation from slavery.

Throughout the Bible there is a tension between this affirmation and empowerment of the weak on the one hand, and a desire to affirm and strengthen the power of the status quo on the other.[4] As male power and domination grow in Israelite society, the side that affirms the status quo becomes more strongly male-oriented and tries more strongly to debase and discount the other. Yet this "other" is never written out of the tradition. This, I think, is what enables both

Jewish and Christian feminism to exist—not in spite of the mono-theism of the tradition but as an integral part of it.

The problem as well as the genius (or inspiration) of monothe-ism is the fact that all aspects of deity are combined in one supreme being. If you live in a polytheistic society, what happens to you can be seen as a reflection of conflicts among deities. When bad things happen, it could mean that another god has temporarily over-whelmed your sponsor. If you are a monotheist, though, any divine struggle has to be a struggle within the one God rather than a struggle among several gods. Any problems are the responsibility of the one deity. If you are suffering, it cannot be because the wrong god won the morning racquetball game; the responsible god is the one you want to think is on your side.

Monotheism taken seriously does not seem to me to support the denigration of women and the feminine. Rather, it is inclusive of all aspects of deity, those traditionally associated with the feminine as well as those traditionally associated with the masculine. The problem with patriarchy in biblical religion (and in the religions derived from the Bible) is that monotheism is not taken seriously enough.

By the end of the Old Testament period (which is probably not long after monolatry gave way to widespread monotheism), there is already an inclination toward dualism. Pseudomonotheism with a dualistic escape clause allows the 'real' god to be responsible only for what one finds good and posits a different god or demigod (the devil in Christian tradition) for what is perceived as wrong or harmful. In effect, it allows two gods, one good and one evil. Nonetheless, it identifies itself as monotheistic because of the claim that, in the end, the good god will triumph over the evil one. It becomes tempting to identify one's enemies with the evil god. Thus, some men have labeled women demonic, some whites have labeled people of color demonic, some Christians have labeled Jews demonic, some Muslims have labeled Christians demonic, some capitalists have labeled socialists demonic, some citizens of develop-ing nations have labeled North Americans demonic, and so on.

If this is correct, it is a mistake to speak of monotheism as essentially a triumph of "male monotheism" over polytheism or goddess religion. "Male" monotheism is itself a failure to take monotheism seriously.

Sex and Gender

There is an important distinction between physical sex and gender. I will use "male" and "female" to refer to sex—that is, physically having male or female sexual characteristics. The primary sex characteristic is the penis or vagina; secondary characteristics include such attributes as a facial beard or developed breasts. (Because the Israelites had no knowledge of X and Y chromosomes, we'll assume that, in their understanding, unless a person had ambiguous genitalia, the person was clearly either male or female.)

Grammatical and Social Gender

Gender can be further subdivided into social gender and grammatical gender. *Social gender*, or what counts as 'socially masculine' or 'socially feminine' can vary from one society to another. In Israelite society as presented by the Bible, among the socially masculine roles were warrior, priest, and heir. Socially feminine roles included, midwife, widow, and prostitute. Such familial roles as mother, son, and wife are also social rather than purely physical constructs. That is, it is possible (through adoption, for example) to relate to someone as 'father' who is not one's biological father. The specific behavior involved in functioning socially as a father or mother may vary from society to society. A behavior that one society considers fatherly may appear motherly in a different society.

In ancient Israel, some socially gendered roles were not absolutely limited to people of the corresponding physical sex. For example, Deborah and Jael were warriors. And Athaliah, while never called "king," reigned for six years after her son's death (2 Kings 11:1-3). According to Numbers 27:1-11, the women Mahlah, Noah, Milcah, Hoglah, and Tirzah, daughters of Zelophehad, set the precedent for women becoming heirs in special circumstances. So a socially masculine or feminine role can be adopted by someone who does not have the appropriate physically male or female identity.

Grammatical gender also varies from one society to another. In English, it is usual to match grammatical gender to physical sex and to use the neuter gender for things without physical sex (and sometimes for babies and animals when one does not know or want to specify sex). In traditional English usage, the grammatical masculine has been used both specifically and generically. That is, sometimes one would use 'he' to indicate a physically male person, while at other times 'he' would be a shorthand way of saying 'person of unspecified sex' or 'any member of a group that includes both males and females.' The grammatical feminine has traditionally been used both to specify females and to personify inanimate beings (e.g., ships) and abstractions (e.g., liberty).

In contemporary usage, many people avoid the use of grammatical gender when physical sex is not being specified. This form of usage results from the awareness that the way we speak both derives from and affects the way we think. When speaking of persons, if we use masculine grammatical forms to mean both 'specifically male' and 'inclusive of males and females' but use feminine grammatical forms only to indicate 'specifically female,' this reflects and reinforces as assumption that the 'normal' human condition is male, and it is 'different' to be female. When we use feminine grammatical forms to indicate both female persons and objects, we reflect and reinforce the idea that a woman is somehow like an object.

In biblical Hebrew, there is no neuter gender. Everything, with or without physical sex, is grammatically masculine or feminine. When speaking of persons and animals, the grammatical gender usually agrees with the physical gender, although in biblical Hebrew, as in traditional English, grammatically masculine forms can be used generically to indicate either 'person of unspecified gender' or 'persons of both genders.' The equivalent of 'she' or 'he' is used of inanimate objects or abstractions, corresponding to their grammatical gender. Generally, biblical personifications follow the grammatical gender, although there are exceptions (e.g., 'Israel' while grammatically masculine, is sometimes personified with masculine and sometimes with feminine imagery).

Biblical Greek does have a neuter gender but ascribes grammatical gender to objects as well as to persons and animals. Again, with persons the grammatical gender usually follows the physical sex, although there are exceptions (e.g., the grammatical gender of child is neuter, whether the child in question is a boy or a girl). In Greek, too, the grammatical masculine gender is used generically to refer to unspecified persons and to groups that include both genders.

The God of the Bible

Male or Female, Masculine or Feminine?

In biblical Hebrew and Greek, references to God use grammatically masculine forms. Because the grammatical masculine can indicate 'person of unspecified sex' as well as 'person of male sex,' grammatical gender alone does not indicate that Yahweh is presented as physically male or even socially masculine.

When God is described in analogies involving social roles, those roles are more often masculine than feminine. (God is presented as father more often than as mother, for example.) Feminine images are possible, although they are less frequent than masculine ones.[5]

Although the Hebrew Bible is fond of anthropomorphic images for God (that is, describing God in terms of human forms), it reveals a reluctance to speak of Yahweh as physically male or female. In part this may be related to the biblical prohibition of images of God. Yahweh is not presented as sexually active in the biblical texts, and there are texts that imply that Yahweh is not male. For example, in Hosea 11:9, when Yahweh says, "I am God and not a man," the word for "man" is not *'adam*, the generic word for "humankind," but *'ish*, a word that refers to an individual person, most often male, that can also be used to mean "husband." Anthropomorphic images are less common in the New Testament than in the Old.

Nevertheless, the biblical tendency is to insist that humans are to relate to God personally, and humans general perceive other persons as gendered individuals. The strong preference for grammatically masculine forms and socially masculine roles would certainly predispose Israelites and early Christians to think of God as at least masculine if not male.

God and Family Images

Some of the most powerful and enduring images used for God in the Bible come from the realm of human relationships. Of these, family relationships are especially important. While I understand these in terms of social gender, surely they also influenced the way Israelites, early Christians, and we have thought of God's physical sex.

God as Father. References to God as father are very common in the

New Testament and also occur in the Old Testament. The uses in the Old Testament emphasize either the closeness of the relationship between Israelites and Yahweh (Isaiah 63:16) or the kinship of Israelites because all relate to the same father (Malachi 2:10).

God as Mother. The image of God as mother occurs in several ways. First, it occurs in similes and other comparisons (Isa. 49:15). In addition, it occurs in metaphors of pregnancy, childbirth, and nursing (Num. 11:12-13; Isa. 42:14).

Ambiguous Parent-Child Images? There are some references to Yahweh as parent that are ambiguous. When God speaks of Israelites as "my children" or of the Israelite king as "my son," the gender of the parent is not explicit. Most intriguing is the reference in Psalm 2, in which Yahweh is quoted as saying to the newly crowned ruler, "You are my son; today I have parented you." Most translations read, "I have begotten you," but the verb form used more often indicates giving birth (the mother's role) than begetting (the father's role).

Of course, either is metaphoric; this is an adoption formula, not a claim of biological parentage. In fact, the adoption concept may be the reason that the specific verb form for "begotten" is not used. Adoptive father is, of course, emphatically a socially masculine role, not a physically male role.

It is important to recognize that people naturally think of personal beings in gendered images. Given the weight of the grammatical gender combined with the overwhelming preference for masculine social gender, it is unlikely that any Israelites took these ambiguous images as anything but "father."

Images of Marriage. In numerous places in the Hebrew Bible (particularly the prophets Hosea, Jeremiah, and Ezekiel), Yahweh is imaged as husband and the people of Israel as wife. The image is most often negative: Israel is an unfaithful wife, Yahweh a patient or angry husband. There are, however, glimpses of the positive side of this image, in which the marriage is a faithful and enduring one (Hosea 2:16-23). In the New Testament, the husband imagery is transferred to Christ, the bride imagery to the church (Eph. 5:22–33).

Yahweh personally is not imaged as the wife of the people or of the faithful individual. However, the image of wife is hinted at for the wisdom of Yahweh. In later Jewish tradition, the Sabbath is imaged as bride. For Jewish mystics, the *shekinah* (the Presence of God) can take on this same image.

Jesus and Father/Son Language. Jesus uses and urges references to God as Father. Yet "father" was not Jesus' only way of speaking about God. Later traditions seem to 'remember' him using father language more frequently than do the earliest ones:

> In the Synoptics, in fact, it is *only* in the Gospel of Matthew that the word "Father" (Greek: *pater*) becomes frequent. It occurs in material particular to Matthew thirty-one times. . . . *Pater* occurs infrequently in the earliest sources, in Mark only four times and in Q nine times in four passages. . . . The idea that the term "Father" was especially central to Jesus' theology and therefore a normative expression for him . . . is not well supported when one looks at the imbalance in the textual referents.[6]

Jesus' usage appears to be related to his specific human family relationships. The biblical tradition of the virgin birth combined with the odd exchange between Mary and Jesus in Luke 2:48b-49[7] and the paucity of later references to Joseph, all combined, may suggest that Jesus did not relate comfortably to Joseph as father. The Gospel of Matthew also recollects that Jesus urged his followers not to relate to any human being as father: "And call no one your father on earth, for you have one Father—the one in heaven" (Matt. 23:9).

Jesus, then, does not seem to use the same relational term for God and for a human being, nor does he urge his followers to use the same term for God and for human fathers. Rather, he urges that this label be reserved for God and denied to humans.

Elisabeth Schüssler Fiorenza understands these father sayings and the "rejection of family" tradition connected with Jesus as a rejection of the patriarchal family.[8] I am not sure that this is the case; if the patriarchal family were the issue, I would expect the directive to abandon "father, mother, son, and daughter" to include husband. But I do think that Jesus shows an awareness of the danger involved in relating to God and humans with the same images—a danger both of reducing God to the level of humans and of elevating humans to the level of God.

Christians as Children of God, Siblings of Christ. The image of the people of God as God's children develops naturally alongside the image of God as father. It derives not only from the Old Testament usage but also from Jesus' urging the use of the "father" address for God and from the analogy of Jesus' relationship with God. It is not a univocal development, though. Sometimes it is an image of all Christians as God's children, and at other times there is a more precise distinction between Jesus' 'real' sonship and the adoption of Christians. At other times, there is a contrast between adopted Christians and natural-born Jews, although family imagery may not be used.

The Wisdom of God

The Wisdom of God in the Hebrew Bible and Apocrypha

Several passages in the Hebrew Bible and in the Apocrypha use the image of wisdom as a woman, or at least as a feminine personal figure. The most significant in the Hebrew Bible are Proverbs 1:20–31, Proverbs 8, and Proverbs 9:1-6. For the heritage of the personification, see also Job 28. In the Apocrypha, add Ben Sira 24 and Wisdom of Solomon 1–8.

If you read through several personification passages hoping to clarify your image of this woman Wisdom, you are likely to be disappointed. In Proverbs 1, she sounds very much like a prophet with one exception: instead of speaking as a messenger of Yahweh, she appears to be speaking from her own authority. In Proverbs 8, Wisdom claims to have been present at creation. In Proverbs 9, she is a woman inviting people to a banquet. The effect of these passages together is not to give a progressively clearer image of Wisdom. Rather, it is like a multiple exposure in which each additional image covers and distorts the others.

For the modern Western reader, questions arise. Who is this Wisdom? What is her heritage? Is she simply a poetic personification of an attribute of Yahweh? Is she a hypostatized attribute of Yahweh—that is, an attribute that has developed into an independent being? Is she a goddess or demi-goddess, the remnant of the Israelite memory of goddess-worship? Does she represent an attempt to co-opt goddess imagery from the surrounding culture without quite admitting to actual goddesses? Or is it rather an attempt to acknowledge the need for feminine images of deity without giving in to polytheism?

No one knows for sure exactly who Wisdom is or how the figure of Wisdom developed. The dating of the Proverbs passages is disputed. It often thought to be post-exilic, but sometimes it is placed instead in pre-exilic Israel, perhaps as early as the age of Solomon (perhaps in the tenth century B.C.E.).

The images of Wisdom in Ben Sira and the Wisdom of Solomon are easier to date (Ben Sira about 225 B.C.E. and Wisdom of Solomon a bit later). They show two developments. Although Wisdom in the Proverbs passages seems to associate with all humankind, in Ben Sira she is identified with Torah and localized in Israel. In the Wisdom of Solomon, she is a link with immortality.

The figure, Woman Wisdom, is described as having been present at creation, either at the first creation or an actual participant in Yahweh's creative process. Other texts that do not clearly personify also speak of Yahweh creating the world "by" or "through" wisdom, and this concept undoubtedly feeds into the personification.

The power and authority of Woman Wisdom (see especially Prov. 1:20-31 and 8:22-31) suggest something more than just an attribute given poetic personification. The theological suggestions that wisdom was present at creation and may even have participated in it suggest something near an independent being.

There are many ways of attempting to account for the figure of Woman Wisdom. One might, for example, assume that Woman Wisdom is presented to a male audience, for whom a woman would be an apt image for wisdom, which is understood to be both valuable and elusive. It is also possible that the image functions partially to compensate for the loss or limitation of female imagery for Yahweh. It could be that the Israelites remembered a time when they were free to worship goddesses. The image may be an accommodation to polytheistic surroundings. This I think less likely. The images of Woman Wisdom become more extravagant in late texts which clearly belong to monotheistic periods. What is striking is that, even at times when Israelites were most concerned about syncretism, they found it permissible to use feminine images in a way that approached suggesting imaging Yahweh as feminine.

None of these attempts is adequate to the power of the texts. There may be more factors to the development of Woman Wisdom than it is possible to identify from our cultural and chronological distance. Even if we could identify her ancestry, though, Woman Wisdom would remain something of a mystery.

Wisdom in the New Testament

In the New Testament, the person of Wisdom is identified with Jesus, sometimes explicitly (1 Cor. 1:24). The personification of wisdom as a woman becomes dissonant with the awareness of Jesus as a male. This dissonance might have been worked out in either of two ways. It might have been possible for the identification of Woman Wisdom with Jesus to open the door to feminine images of Christ. Or such an identification could serve to close the door to feminine personifications of wisdom. I find it unfortunate that the latter is the way things developed.

It may be partially because of the dissonance between feminine Wisdom and male Jesus that a companion attribute, the Word or Logos, is also developed. The Greek *logos* is grammatically masculine and thus more easily harmonized with personification in the person of Jesus. In western Christian tradition, the personification of Wisdom becomes rare (although occasionally the imagery of wisdom is applied to Mary) and the personification of Logos as Jesus takes over.

The Spirit of God

Range of Meaning

In both Hebrew and Greek, the word for "spirit" has a wide range of meanings—breath and wind, for example, as well as spirit. Generally speaking, the Hebrew Bible uses "spirit of God" to refer to an aspect or attribute of God or to image God's breath metaphorically. The spirit is what comes upon Yahweh's chosen leaders, especially prophets or judges. It is a divine gift enabling them both to lead and to experience the divine word or will in particular ways. Spirit is also what makes living beings alive. In Genesis 2, God forms a creature out of clay, but it is not a living being until God breathes spirit into it. Similarly, in Ezekiel 37, dry bones in a valley come together into human forms and are even covered with muscles and sinews and skin, but they are not alive until Yahweh has the prophet call the wind from the four corners of the earth and blow spirit into them.

In the New Testament, sometimes the connection of "spirit" with "breath" is explicit. An example is John 20:22: "When [Jesus] had said this, he breathed on [the disciples] and said to them, 'Receive the Holy Spirit.'" The connection with wind can be explicit too, as in Jesus' conversation with Nicodemus in John 3. At other times in the New Testament, the Spirit of God is that about God or Christ which is with Christians after Jesus is physically gone. The Spirit is particularly seen as a special endowment connected with the holiday of Pentecost.

Spirit as Persona

In Hebrew, the possibility of imaging spirit in human terms is largely feminine because the word *ruach* is grammatically feminine. But the Greek word *pneuma* is grammatically neuter, so the possibility exists for either feminine or masculine personification. In later Christian tradition, masculine images prevail. Clearly, though, there is no biblical reason for limiting spirit language to the masculine.

The Hebrew Bible does not contain the concept of the Spirit of God as a distinct persona, certainly not as a member of the Trinity, because the idea of the Trinity had not yet been developed. There are times in the New Testament when the Spirit is imaged as an independent, personal being (e.g., the Advocate, John 14:16-17, 26; the Spirit interceding for Christians, Rom. 8:26).

With the development of the doctrine of the Trinity, Spirit is more frequently (although not always) personified in masculine terms. This may be partly unreflective, coming from the patriarchal assumption that the 'normal' personal condition is male, and female is special, a difference. It may be in part an attempt to avoid the possibility of thinking of sexual activity among the persons of the godhead. It may also be influenced by the masculine gender of the Latin word *spiritus*.

How Shall We Speak About God?

Biblical Images: Implications

The total picture of these family images suggests a predominant image of God as socially masculine. The most significant breaks in this picture come in the images of Yahweh as mother, in the personifications of wisdom, and in the openness of spirit to feminine imagery.

To me, these breaks, however infrequent, suggest two things. First, there is within some strains of the tradition an awareness that masculine imagery does not cover the whole range of what it means to be God. Therefore, I take the feminine images as a tribute to the monotheism of the Bible rather than as a concession to polytheism. Second, the one feminine image that is used directly of Yahweh, however hesitantly, is "mother." This is also the one feminine role in patriarchal society in which it is usual for women to have authority over males. Thus, a factor in the refusal to image Yahweh as a woman may be the lack of authority that women had in the culture and the insistence on Yahweh's own authority.

God and Gender Today

The way we think about gender issues in the late-twentieth-century Western world is something that would not have occurred to the Israelites or early Christians. Although some Israelites probably avoided talking about Yahweh as a sexual being, to maintain the distinctiveness of Yahwism from surrounding religions, neither they nor early Christians would have contemplated the implications of speaking of gender in reference to God. Some of the questions that may be important to us were simply not on their cultural agenda.

We, however, can hardly avoid thinking about gender issues. In recent decades, traditional masculine and feminine roles have been radically redefined. In particular, the assumptions of patriarchy have been challenged. No longer can we suppose that the normal human condition is male/masculine, and that female/feminine experience is simply an aberration. No longer can we assume that every household is headed by a male, or that women can be kept in a state of perpetual dependency.

In addition, social and linguistic developments in our own time challenge our ways of thinking and talking about God. Many speakers of English today, unlike those of previous generations, make a deliberate effort to distinguish between terms that mean 'specifically male' and words that mean 'personal but sex not specified.' I applaud this effort, as it undercuts the assumptions that maleness or masculinity is normative humanity. At the same time, it complicates our talking about God. When we use the grammatical masculine only for males in our speech about people but continue to use exclusively masculine terms when we refer to God, we cannot help giving the impression that God actually is, if not physically male, at least socially masculine.

The question of gender and God is neither a trivial nor a purely personal one. It is not simply a matter of "How would I like to think about God?" Rather, it is a profoundly theological question. The exclusive use of unreflective masculine language is no longer a responsible act.[9] Given the state of our language today, we must make a decision. Biblical theologians must consider what is said about God in the Bible (both testaments). We must ask about both the origin and the purpose of the preference for masculine language and images. Is God depicted through masculine language because (1) the shapers of the biblical texts were so thoroughly male-oriented that they could not conceive of any other possibility? Does the usage indicate that (2) in the ancient Israelite and early Christian cultural settings, it was necessary to depict God as socially masculine? Or (3) is there something in the nature of God that makes it necessary to depict God as socially masculine in all cultural settings—or at least in our own?

I am convinced that the biblical usage reflects both the concerns of the groups responsible for transmitting the texts and the social setting in which they lived. In a male-centered culture, it is natural to think first of male and masculine images. In a culture in which men had almost all positions of authority (if a woman did hold such a position, she was taking on a socially masculine role), it is natural to think of God in male and masculine terms. I believe that these terms were used because of the cultural settings in which the Bible developed and not because of an inherent maleness or masculinity in God.

Given the male orientation of biblical cultures, the amazing thing is that there are any feminine images for God. To me, their existence suggests a willingness to take monotheism seriously, to recognize that a god who incorporates only the masculine aspects of deity is not a full reflection of the divine.

In the usage of the church, the Bible's masculine images for God have been appropriated and developed, while its feminine images have minimized. Churches that use the common lectionary never hear most of the texts that present the possibility of the feminine within God. People who know the Bible through the Sunday lectionary readings have less access to feminine imagery than did either ancient Israelites or early Christians.

Very few adult Christians or Jews today would claim that God is physically male. And yet, the traditional use of exclusively masculine grammatical references and primarily masculine images predispose us to think of God as socially masculine. Because we have inherited the biblical tradition of relating to God personally, and because we perceive persons as male or female, thinking of God as socially masculine means that we are likely to image God as physically male, even if we do claim that physical maleness is not an aspect of God's being.

For me, it is not only possible but important to use both feminine and masculine images to refer to God. In our cultural and linguistic setting, this is the most effective way of encouraging personal relationship with God without promoting the idea that God is male.

Varying Our Relational Analogies

The difficulty with translating relational metaphors is that one has not only to get the words right but also to understand what the relationship indicated to its original audience. If I am correct that "father" is not primarily a biological but a social term, and the specifics of the social relationship can vary from one culture to another, in order to understand what is being said about God by "father" we must understand not primarily who a father is biologically but what a father does relationally. When Jesus called "father," was he claiming the same kind of relationship that we identify with the word "father" today? Is some of the relationship Jesus claimed more appropriate for "mother" today? I believe it is. With the increasing technologizing of western society, fathers have become increasingly remote. It is not, I think, accidental that the God addressed as "father" also grew more remote through the centuries. For this reason (among others), I consider it a mistake to make "father" the paradigmatic label for God.

Yet I am not urging that "mother" become our usual label for God. The combination of Jesus' usage with his warnings about using father language about humans suggests that he may have been aware of dangers in the use of a single term of address for both God and humans—dangers of either idolizing humans or reducing the divine to human scale. For that reason, it seems to me inappropriate for people, claiming the command or at least permission of Jesus, to use as their primary address to God the term that they also use for the men who function as fathers in their lives. It seems equally inappropriate to use as their primary address to God the term that they use for the women who function as mothers in their lives.

I do not think it good to eliminate father images entirely. It might be an appropriate move, however, to (1) retain for most corporate use the Aramaic 'abba, which Christians generally do not use of people, and/or (2) for private devotional use to use a father term that one does not use for one's own father. The word 'abba is not the formal word "father" but an affectionate term used in family relationships. One might try using such a word—perhaps "Papa" or "Daddy"—preferably a term which clearly indicates a relationship but not the word one uses for one's own father. I would urge the same caution in the use of mother language. If as a child you called your mother "Mommy," try "Mama" for God.

I do not want to eliminate the use of parent images, but I do not think they should be our only images of relationships with God. Parent-child images are beautifully comforting but do nothing to encourage Christians to 'grow up' in the faith. It is worthwhile to develop more of the variety of biblical usage.

Another possibility for private use is to understand Jesus' directive as urging the use of a label which indicates a close relationship we desire but do not have among humans. For example, Brian Wren notes that "sister" is meaningful to him, but offensive to some people for whom it resonates too strongly with a negative experience with a human sister.[10] I have the same sense. Having no sisters, I can easily idealize a sister relationship. The meaning is not muddied for me the way "father," "mother," and "brother" are by the experiences I have had in my own human family. Similarly, single people might find spouse language more appropriate than married people do. (Is it accidental that Paul, who developed the Bride of Christ image for the church, was unmarried?)

I wonder, too, whether the affection for the term "father" in relation to God in Western tradition is related to a distancing of human fathers from their children. Could it be that generations of children have grown up longing for the presence of a father who is not there physically or emotionally and have loved addressing God as "father" because it allows God to fill a gap in their human relationships? In my own limited experience, it seems that the people who find it essential to relate to God as "father" are often those who either do not know their fathers or do not have close, loving relationships with them.

These reflections are offered not as a prescription but in order to encourage you to explore the possibilities. If there is a relationship you long for but do not have, try it out in prayer. See what happens. If your understanding of God cannot fit the image, try another. Given the variety of linguistic images for God in the Bible, I do not think there are many that must be rejected before they are tried.

Although most of the suggestions here are directed toward private devotions, they can also shape the ways in which communities speak of God. Corporate worship is both enriched and complicated by the variety of experiences and needs that are represented in the group. There are those whose language about God is open to traditional, forgotten, and innovative images. But for a variety of reasons, there are some people who cannot relate to God with traditional language and others who cannot relate to God without it. How can one community enable the worship of all these groups?

When worship is absolutely consistent, it will drive out one group or another. With variety and flexibility within the framework provided by the Bible and the church, as many as possible will be enabled to worship meaningfully. I urge variety, conversation, and love.

Notes

Chapter 1—Women's Roles: Historical Reconstruction

1. Denise Carmody, *Biblical Woman: Contemporary Reflections on Scriptural Texts* (New York: Crossroad, 1989), 39.

2. Unless otherwise indicated, biblical quotations follow the New Revised Standard Version (NRSV) with one exception: where the Hebrew text has the proper name of God, Yahweh, which is rendered "the LORD" in most translations, including the NRSV, I have used "Yahweh" instead.

3. Judith Romney Wegner, "Deuteronomy," in *The Women's Bible Commentary*, ed. Carol A. Newsom and Sharon H. Ringe (Louisville, KY: Westminster/John Knox, 1992), 98.

4. The first reference is in "Hymn of Victory of Mer-ne-Ptah (The Israel Stele)," in *Ancient Near Eastern Texts Relating to the Old Testament*, 3d with supp., ed. James B. Pritchard (Princeton: Princeton University Press, 1969), 376-78.

5. The differentiation of two types of prophecy comes from Robert R. Wilson, *Prophecy and Society in Ancient Israel* (Philadelphia: Fortress, 1980). Wilson, however, does observe both types of prophecy in both north and south.

6. Carol Meyers, *Discovering Eve: Ancient Israelite Women in Context* (Oxford: Oxford University Press, 1988). See especially 168-73 and 188-94.

7. The 40 percent figure may be surprising: why not 50 percent? Because women are always responsible for childbearing and usually responsible for most early child care, when everyone is working at full potential women's economic contribution is about 40 percent. When they contribute either more or less, their status declines.

8. Judith Romney Wegner, *Chattel or Person? The Status of Women in the Mishnah* (New York: Oxford University Press, 1988), 14.

9. According to levirate law as described in Deut. 25:5-10, if a married man died childless, his brother was to marry the widow; their first child was to "succeed to the name of the deceased brother, so that

his name may not be blotted out of Israel." The biblical narratives that reflect levirate law (Gen. 38; Ruth) assume that it is applicable to relatives other than the brother of the deceased. While the law is designed to protect men's property and status, in a society organized around the extended household it would also have been important to maintain the woman's place and survival.

10. The role of adult daughter is not explicit in the Bible, but Wegner believes that "the restriction of the father's authority to the case of a *minor* daughter necessarily implies" it. In the Mishnah (later Jewish law codified about 200 C.E.), a woman was legally emancipated if her father had not arranged her marriage by the age of twelve and one-half and one day (Wegner, *Chattel or Person*, 14–15).

11. The relationship between Sarah and Hagar is discussed in chapter 2. For an alternative reconstruction of these two women, see Savina J. Teubel, *Sarah the Priestess* (Athens, OH: Swallow Press, 1984) and *Hagar the Egyptian: The Lost Tradition of the Matriarchs* (San Francisco: Harper & Row, 1990).

12. It is important to distinguish between "patriarch" as remembered ancestors and "patriarchy" as a social system of male power enforced through "the fathers." The time of the ancestors is often called the "patriarchal period" in the first sense, but it is not the most "patriarchal" in the second sense.

13. In fact, Carol Meyers suggests plausibly that Rebekah rather than Isaac is really the hero of these stories. See "'To Her Mother's House': Considering a Counterpart to the Israelite *Bêt 'ab*," in *The Bible and the Politics of Exegesis*, ed. David Jobling, Peggy Day, and Gerald T. Sheppard (Cleveland: The Pilgrim Press, 1989), 42–44.

14. This is a matter of social standing, as her father is born to Nahor's principal wife.

15. Although this might be inserted simply for the sake of parallelism, it does not occur in comparable Egyptian instructions which also use poetic parallelism.

16. This comparison comes from Claudia V. Camp, "1 and 2 Kings," in *The Women's Bible Commentary*, 98.

17. Tikva S. Frymer-Kensky, "Women," in *Harper's Bible Dictionary* (San Francisco: Harper & Row, 1985), 1139.

18. Athalya Brenner notes that while the normative tradition rejects magic in general, it does include some magical elements. See *The Israelite Woman: Social Role and Literary Type in Biblical Narrative*, The Biblical Seminar (Sheffield: JSOT Press, 1985), 69–70.

19. This is suggested by S. D. Goitein on the basis of biblical references observations of Yemeni immigrants to Israel and comparisons with ancient Arabic poetry. See "Woman as Creators of Biblical Genres," *Prooftexts* 8 (1988): 1–33.

20. Brenner, *The Israelite Woman*, 46–50.

21. Harold Bloom, *The Book of J*, trans. David Rosenberg, interpr. Harold Bloom (New York: Grove, Weidenfeld, 1990).

22. This distinguishes Hebrew alphabetic writing from the more complicated systems of Egyptian hieroglyphics and Akkadian cuneiform. To use those systems, a scribe had to learn hundreds of signs; to read and write Hebrew, a person needed to learn only twenty-two letters. There is, then, the potential for widespread literacy in Israelite culture, although the use of writing was probably limited to those who felt a need for it.

23. This reconstruction is from Carol L. Meyers, "Everyday Life: Women in the Period of the Hebrew Bible," in *The Women's Bible Commentary*, 246–47.

24. Wegner, "Deuteronomy," 59–60.

25. This is my own literal translation of the Hebrew.

26. So NRSV, Tanakh, TEV. One need not argue with "wife," since the Hebrew word for "woman" is also the usual word for "wife" (just as the Hebrew word for "man" is also used for "husband"), and the woman presented here is clearly married. The adjective is the sticking point.

27. "Her lamp does not go out" may indicate that she is working late into the night, but it may also be an indication of her prosperity: there is never any danger of running out of lamp oil in this household.

28. While the NRSV takes this as a simile ("She is like the ships of the merchant"), it is also possible to translate this line as a reference to actual involvement with merchant ships.

29. This is a literal rendering. Commentators make sense of it by making "fear of Yahweh" a characteristic of the woman, but this could more easily be expressed in other ways.

30. On the personifications, see the discussion in chapter 6.

Chapter 2—Women and Women: Dynamic Analogy

1. The method as described here is developed from James Sanders's description of dynamic analogy as an interpretive method of canonical criticism in *Canon and Community: A Guide to Canonical Criticism*, Guides to Biblical Scholarship, Old Testament Series (Philadelphia: Fortress, 1984), especially 70-71.

2. The NRSV, following the Greek and Latin versions, adds "With her son Isaac," which is not in the Hebrew text and not assumed in my reading.

3. On the question of Yahweh's gender, see chapter 6. My judgment here is about Hagar's perception, not Yahweh's identity.

4. E. A. Speiser, trans., "The Legend of Sargon," in *Ancient Near Eastern Texts*, 119.

5. See especially Susan Niditch, "Eroticism and Death in the Tale of Jael," in *Gender and Difference in Ancient Israel*, ed. Peggy L. Day (Minneapolis: Fortress, 1989). An analysis which combines awareness of the erotic with awareness of maternal images is Danna Nolan Fewell and David M. Gunn, "Controlling Perspectives: Women, Men, and the Authority of Violence in Judges 4 and 5," *Journal of the American Academy of Religion* 58 (1990): 389-411.

6. Fewell and Gunn, "Controlling Perspectives," 407.

7. This is my own translation, designed to bring out the play on words between "Naomi" (which means "sweet") and "Mara" ("bitter").

8. According to the levirate law in Deuteronomy, if a married man died childless, his brother was obligated to marry the widow to provide offspring for the dead man. Laws similar but not identical to the one in Deuteronomy are assumed by both this story and that of Tamar and Judah (see chapter 3).

9. These parallels are described by Craig A. Evans, *Luke*, New International Biblical Commentary (Peabody, MA: Hendrickson, 1990), 22-23. Only 1-9 are present in this portion of the narrative.

10. The surprise of Elizabeth's response and her social "right" to resent Mary and deny the younger woman's joy is explored sensitively by Renita J. Weems. See "Unbegrudged Blessings," in *Just a Sister Away: A Womanist Vision of Women's Relationships in the Bible* (San Diego: LuraMedia, 1988), 113-126, especially 121.

Chapter 3—Women and Men: Hermeneutic of Suspicion

1. This understanding is contrary to that of Esther Fuchs, who is suspicious of the fact that, in the stories of both Tamar and Ruth, women are presented as supporting the levirate system, which is designed to protect men's interests in inheritance and male offspring and doing so out of self-seeking motives. She claims, "By projecting onto woman what man desires most, the biblical narrative creates womanhood in its own image" ("The Literary Characterization of Mothers and Sexual Politics in the Hebrew Bible," *Semeia* 46 [1989]: 161). In contrast, it seems to me that, in a society based on the male-headed household, the social advantages of living within the system are not figments of the male imagination.

2. Fokkelien van Dijk-Hemmes, "Tamar and the Limits of Patriarchy: Between Rape and Seduction (2 Samuel 13 and Genesis 38)," in *Anti-Covenant: Counter-Reading Women's Lives in the Hebrew Bible*, ed. Mieke Bal, Bible and Literature Series 22, JSOT Supplement 81 (Sheffield, England: Almond, 1989), 149.

3. Dijk-Hemmes, "Tamar and the Limits of Patriarchy," 151.

4. In contrast, Gerhard von Rad claims that "the story of Judah and Tamar has no connection at all with the strictly organized Joseph story." See *Genesis: A Commentary*, Old Testament Library (Philadelphia: Westminster, 1961), 356.

5. "Leprous" here and elsewhere in the Bible indicates some kind of abnormal skin condition but not the disease that we know as leprosy today.

6. Martin Noth, *Numbers: A Commentary*, Old Testament Library (Philadelphia: Westminster, 1968), 92-93.

7. Rita Burns, *Has the Lord Indeed Spoken Only Through Moses? A Study of the Biblical Portrait of Miriam* (Atlanta: Scholars Press, 1987).

8. Ibid.

9. There are seven texts that explicitly refer to Miriam: Exod.15:20-21; Num. 12; Num. 20:1; Num. 26:59; Deut. 24:9; 1 Chron. 6:3; and Mic. 6:4. The only one that describes leadership behavior is the first. According to Exod. 15:20-21, Miriam led the women in song and dance after the crossing of the Reed Sea. This passage also calls Miriam a prophet.

10. This likelihood is discounted by Noth, *Numbers*, 94.

11. Katharine Doob Sakenfeld, "Numbers," in *The Women's Bible Commentary*, 48.

12. Phyllis Trible, "Bringing Miriam Out of the Shadows," *Bible Review* 5, no. 1 (February 1989): 23.

13. Jo Ann Hackett, "1 and 2 Samuel," in *The Women's Bible Commentary*, 92. Hackett notes that Saul had a wife named Ahinoam and that in a later oracle Nathan quotes Yahweh as telling David, "I rescued you from the hand of Saul; I gave you your master's house, and your master's wives into your bosom."

14. For a brief discussion of the power of the queen mother, see Camp, "1 and 2 Kings," in *The Women's Bible Commentary*, 98.

15. This is pointed out by Joel Rosenberg, "The Institutional Matrix of Treachery in 2 Samuel 11," *Semeia* 46 (1989): 105.

16. Richard D. Nelson, *First and Second Kings*, Interpretation: A Bible Commentary for Teaching and Preaching (Atlanta: John Knox Press, 1987), 110.

17. The longer ending of Mark includes the report that "those who had been with" Jesus did not believe Mary Magdalene when she told them that Jesus was alive and that she had seen him (Mark 16:10-11).

    The ending of Mark has a complicated tradition. The undisputed portion of the book ends with verse 8, in which the women "said nothing to anyone, for they were afraid." There are two alternate endings, one short and one long; manuscripts differ in whether they include one or the other or both. For the purposes of this chapter, I will use the undisputed portion (ending with verse 8) as Mark's account, although I will note information from the two endings in notes.

18. The undisputed part of Mark has no resurrection appearances at all. A number of appearances, including one to Mary Magdalene (16:9) are reported in the longer ending of Mark.

19. Pheme Perkins, "'I Have Seen the Lord' (John 20:18): Women Witnesses to the Resurrection," *Interpretation* 46 (1992): 34.

20. Ibid., 35.

21. Ibid.

22. Ibid., 38.

23. Mary Rose D'Angelo, in her study of the redaction of Luke ("Women in Luke-Acts: A Redactional View," *Journal of Biblical Literature* 109 [1990]: 441-61), contrasts the favorable treatment of Luke by Constance Parvey ("The Theology and Leadership of Women in the New Testament," in *Religion and Sexism*, ed. Rosemary Radford Ruether [New York: Simon & Schuster, 1974], 139-46) with more recent studies emphasizing Luke's androcentrism, especially Elisabeth Schüssler Fiorenza, "A Feminist Critical Interpretation for Liberation: Martha and Mary: Luke 10:38-42," *Religion and Intellectual Life* 3 (1986): 21-35.

24. Jane Schaberg points out that, although the gospel of Luke includes many stories of women ("forty-two passages of which twenty-three are unique to Luke"), the women in Luke are limited to roles that would be acceptable to imperial Rome. (See "Luke," in *The Women's Bible Commentary*, 279).

25. D'Angelo, "Women in Luke-Acts," 452.

26. Ibid., 461.

27. Elisabeth Schüssler Fiorenza, *In Memory of Her: A Feminist Theological Reconstruction of Christian Origins* (New York: Crossroad/ Continuum, 1983), 167.

28. Gail R. O'Day, "Acts," in *The Women's Bible Commentary*, 309.

29. Ibid., 310.

Chapter 4—Women and Jesus: Reading from Below

1. Judith Plaskow, "Feminist Anti-Judaism and the Christian God," *Journal of Feminist Studies in Religion* 7, no. 2 (Fall 1991): 104.

2. O'Day, "John," in *The Women's Bible Commentary*, 295.

3. Ibid., 297.

4. Sharon H. Ringe, "A Gentile Woman's Story," in *Feminist Interpretation of the Bible*, ed. Letty M. Russell (Philadelphia: Westminster, 1985), 65-72.

   The interpretation offered in this section follows that of Paul S. Minear in "Writing on the Ground: The Puzzle in John 8:1-11," *Horizons in Biblical Theology* 13 (1991): 23-27.

5. Mary Rose D'Angelo, "Women Partners in the New Testament," *Journal of Feminist Studies in Religion* 6, no. 1 (Spring 1990): 77-81.

6. For example, Schaberg, "Luke," in *The Women's Bible Commentary*, 289.

7. Fiorenza, *In Memory of Her*, xiii. This story provides the title for the book.

8. "A Nicaraguan Example: The Alabaster Bottle. Matthew 26:6-13," in *Voices from the Margin: Interpreting the Bible in the Third World*, ed. R. S. Sugirtharajah, (Maryknoll, NY: Orbis, 1991), 412-19.

9. Ibid., 412.

10. Ibid., 417.

11. Ibid., 418.

12. Ibid., 418-19.

13. Perkins, "I Have Seen the Lord," 36.

14. According to Pheme Perkins, "The absence of any reaction of fear makes it unlikely that John thought of the story as an angelophany" (*Resurrection: New Testament Witness and Contemporary Reflection* [Garden City, NY: Doubleday, 1984], 175).

15. Ibid. 175-76; Perkins cites 3:13; 6:62; 7:33; 13:1, 3; 14:4, 28; 16:5, 17, 28; and 17:13.

16. The word the NRSV translates as "bridesmaids" is literally "virgins."

17. Plaskow, "Feminist Anti-Judaism," especially 104 and 106.

Chapter 5—Women in the Garden: Interpreting the Tradition

1. See Job 38-42 (particularly Job 38); Ps. 104; Prov. 8:22-31, and Isa. 40:12-14, 45:5-7, 11-12. These texts suggest ways of talking about creation using primarily two groups of images—architecture and battle. Neither image group is prominent in the Genesis texts, although architecture is hinted at in Gen. 2:22. For a treatment of creation with emphasis on the non-Genesis texts, see Jon Levenson, *Creation and the Persistence of Evil: The Jewish Drama of Divine Omnipotence* (San Francisco: Harper & Row, 1988).

2. This is new with the Hebrews. Like other ancient semitic peoples, the Hebrews celebrated moon phases (especially the new moon and full moon), but for them, the rhythm of these moon phases was subordinated to the rhythm of the seven-day week, which initially approximates the phases of the moon but soon falls out of synchronization with them.

3. NRSV reads "a helper as his partner." It has been widely pointed out in recent scholarship that "helper" (Hebrew '*ezer)* does not imply "inferior," and humans in fact refer to God as "helper" (Exod. 18:4; Deut. 33:7,26; Ps. 33:20; 70:5; 115:9, 10, 11; 146:5).

4. All of these claims (the earthling is ungendered until the surgery; creation last does not indicate subordination; naming of the woman does not occur until Gen. 3:20) are made by Phyllis Trible in her formalist reading of the Eden story, "A Love Story Gone Awry," in *God and the Rhetoric of Sexuality,* Overtures to Biblical Theology (Philadelphia: Fortress Press, 1978), 72-143. Susan S. Lanser challenges Trible's reading on the basis of speech-act theory ("[Feminist] Criticism in the Garden: Inferring Genesis 2-3," *Semeia* 41 [1988)] 67-84). The differing conclusions are possible in part because Trible focuses on what is formally present in the text and Lanser on what she surmises would "go without saying" in a typical speech event. A problem in evaluating Lanser's claims is our culture's limited information about ancient Israelite cultural conventions. It is often impossible to be sure what would go without saying.

5. This is in the Hebrew text and, although it is in the NRSV, it has not been included in most translations

6. The messianic understanding of Gen. 3:15 comes from a stage of interpretation which identifies the serpent with the Devil.

7. Meyers, *Discovering Eve*, 75.

8. The first of these is probably Sirach 25:24 (dated to about 200 B.C.E.): "From a woman sin had its beginning/ and because of her we all die." Cited by Meyers, *Discovering Eve*.

9. Ibid.

10. Ibid., 117-21.

11. Most translations, including the NRSV, have "husband" instead of "man." The Hebrew word can be used for either.

12. Phyllis Trible offers such a reading in "Love's Lyrics Redeemed," in *God and the Rhetoric of Sexuality*, 144-65.

13. Marvin Pope provides a summary of the proposals in *The Song of Solomon: A Commentary*, Anchor Bible vol. 7C (Garden City NY: Doubleday, 1977), 34-37, 40-54.

14. The refrains, themes, and motifs cited here are those noted by Roland E. Murphy, (*The Song of Songs*, Hermeneia—A Critical and Historical Commentary on the Bible [Minneapolis: Fortress Press, 1990], 76-80), although the translations follow the NRSV except as noted.

15. This is my own translation. NRSV translates it as a wish ("O that his left hand were . . . "), and Murphy (*The Song of Songs*) translates it as a description ("His left hand is . . ."). The only verb in the Hebrew ("embracing") is a participle, and thus tense is not indicated.

16. The NRSV translates this expression as "What is that" in 3:6, "Who is this" in 6:10, and "Who is that" in 8:5; the Hebrew phrase is the same in all three verses.

17. This speculation is noted by Renita J. Weems, "Song of Songs," in *The Women's Bible Commentary*, 157.

18. See note 15.

19. In the study of Near Eastern texts, this kind of descriptive motif is called a *wasf*, named first for later Arabic poems.

20. Woman's "entrance into a dominant scopic economy signifies, once again, her relegation to passivity: she will be the beautiful object." Luce Irigaray, untitled essay in *New French Feminisms: An Anthology*, ed. E. Marks and I. de Coutirron (New York: Schocken, 1981).

21. A very different way of reading this particular *wasf* is offered by Athalya Brenner in "'Come Back, Come Back the Shulammite' (Song of Songs 7.1-10): A Parody of the *Wasf* Genre," in *On Humour and the Comic in the Hebrew Bible*, Bible and Literature Series 23, JSOT Supplement Series 92, ed. Yehuda T. Radday and Athalya Brenner (Sheffield, England: Almond Press, 1990), 251–75. As the title indicates, Brenner understands this poem as a parody.

22. The term *shahebet-ya* (8:6) translates literally to "flame of Yah." Many interpreters understand it as an intensifier (the NRSV as "a raging flame") rather than as a consciously religious reference.

23. The NRSV has "he pastures his flock among the lilies." "His flock" is not in the Hebrew.

24. This imagery is found, for example, in Isa. 5:1-4.

25. Such efforts are outlined by Pope in his Anchor Bible commentary. In sacred marriage rituals, a human couple enacts a sexual relationship understood to take place in the divine realm, for the apparent purpose of ensuring fertility during the coming year.

26. For a treatment of this control in later Jewish law, Talmud (a tradition in continuity with that of the Bible, although at least several hundred years later than this text), see Wegner, *Chattel or Person?* Wegner finds that the Talmud treats women as persons in most areas, but in regard to their sexuality treats them as chattels, and she traces the origins of this understanding to the Bible.

27. Michael V. Fox, *The Song of Songs and the Ancient Egyptian Love Songs* (Madison: University of Wisconsin Press, 1985) understands the Egyptian word to mean "diversion" and suggests that the Song of Songs "too was probably entertainment" (247).

28. Ibid., 251.

29. Ibid., 237.

30. Pope, *Song of Songs*, 158-78.

31. Contrast the imagery of Hos. 1-2, Ezek. 16.

32. Trible, "Love's Lyrics Redeemed."

Chapter 6—Gender and God: Constructive Biblical Theology

1. See Saul M. Olyan, *Asherah and the Cult of Yahweh in Israel*, SBL Monograph Series, 34 (Atlanta: Scholars Press, 1988).

2. Sanders, *Canon and Community*.

3. This specific commandment might forbid only the worship of other deities in shrines of Yahweh or might forbid that Hebrews worship other deities at all. Either way, it regulates what the Hebrews are allowed to *do* and does not make a theological claim about the *existence* of other gods.

4. This tension is outlined by Walter Brueggemann, "A Shape for Biblical Theology, I: Structure and Legitimation" and "A Shape for Biblical Theology, II: Embrace of Pain," in Patrick D. Miller, ed., *Old Testament Theology: Essays on Structure, Theme, and Text* (Minneapolis: Fortress Press, 1992), 1–44.

5. Virginia Ramey Mollenkott identifies images of God as mother (giving birth, nursing, nurturing), midwife, mother bear, female homemaker, female beloved, bakerwoman, mother hen, and Dame Wisdom (*The Divine Feminine: The Biblical Imagery of God as Female* [New York: Crossroad, 1989]). The variety of mother images, in particular, is surprising. Mollenkott's treatment is hardly cautious: she gives the benefit of the doubt to the female/feminine, just as traditional theology has to the male/masculine.

6. Susan Brooks Thistlethwaite, "On the Trinity," *Interpretation* 45 (1991): 161-62.

7. Mary: "Child, why have you treated us like this? Look, your father and I have been searching for you in great anxiety." Jesus: "Why were you searching for me? Did you not know that I must be in my Father's house?"

8. Fiorenza, *In Memory of Her*, 140-51.

9. Note "unreflective." It is different when people reflect on the concepts and their implications and conclude that God really is socially masculine in our society. I disagree with this theology but respect it as responsible.

10. Brian Wren, *What Language Shall I Borrow? God-Talk in Worship: A Male Response to Feminist Theology* (New York: Crossroad, 1990), 164.

Selected Bibliography

Bal, Mieke, ed. *Anti-Covenant: Counter-Reading Women's Lives in the Hebrew Bible*. Bible and Literature Series 22. JSOT Supplement 81. Sheffield, England: Almond Press, 1989.

Bloom, Harold. *The Book of J*. New York: Grove, Weidenfeld, 1990.

Brenner, Athalya. *The Israelite Woman: Social Role and Literary Type in Biblical Narrative*. The Biblical Seminar: Sheffield, England: JSOT Press, 1985.

Burns, Rita. *Has the Lord Indeed Spoken Only Through Moses? A Study of the Biblical Portrait of Miriam*. Atlanta: Scholars Press, 1987.

Carmody, Denise. *Biblical Woman: Contemporary Reflections on Scriptural Texts*. New York: Crossroad, 1989.

Day, Peggy L., ed. *Gender and Difference in Ancient Israel*. Minneapolis: Fortress Press, 1989.

Evans, Craig A. *Luke*. New International Biblical Commentary. Peabody, MA: Hendrickson, 1990.

Fiorenza, Elisabeth Schüssler. *In Memory of Her: A Feminist Theological Reconstruction of Christian Origins*. New York: Crossroad/Continuum, 1983.

Fox, Michael V. *The Song of Songs and the Ancient Egyptian Love Songs*. Madison: University of Wisconsin Press, 1985.

Jobling, David, Peggy Day, and Gerald T. Sheppard, eds. *The Bible and the Politics of Exegesis*. Cleveland: The Pilgrim Press, 1991.

Levenson, Jon. *Creation and the Persistence of Evil: The Jewish Drama of Divine Omnipotence*. San Francisco: Harper & Row, 1988.

Marks, E., and I. de Coutirron, eds. *New French Feminisms: An Anthology*. New York: Schocken, 1981.

Meyers, Carol. *Discovering Eve: Ancient Israelite Women in Context*. Oxford: Oxford University Press, 1988.

Mollenkott, Virginia Ramey. *The Divine Feminine: The Biblical Imagery of God as Female*. New York: Crossroad, 1989.

Murphy, Roland E. *The Song of Songs*. Hermeneia–A Critical and Historical Commentary on the Bible. Minneapolis: Fortress Press, 1990.

Nelson, Richard D. *First and Second Kings*. Interpretation: A Bible Commentary for Teaching and Preaching. Atlanta: John Knox Press, 1987.

Newsom, Carol A., and Sharon H. Ringe, eds. *The Women's Bible Commentary*. Louisville, KY: Westminster/John Knox, 1992.

Noth, Martin. *Numbers: A Commentary*. Old Testament Library. Philadelphia: Westminster, 1968.

Olyan, Saul M. *Asherah and the Cult of Yahweh in Israel*. Society for Biblical Literature Monograph Series 34. Atlanta: Scholars Press, 1988.

Perkins, Pheme. *Resurrection: New Testament Witness and Contemporary Reflections*. Garden City, NY: Doubleday, 1984.

Pope, Marvin. *The Song of Solomon: A Commentary*. Anchor Bible, vol. 7C. Garden City, NY: Doubleday, 1977.

Pritchard, James B., ed. *Ancient Near Eastern Texts Relating to the Old Testament*. 3d ed. Princeton: Princeton University Press, 1969.

Rad, Gerhard von. *Genesis: A Commentary*. Old Testament Library. Philadelphia: Westminster, 1991.

Radday, Yehuda T., and Athalya Brenner, eds. *On Humour and the Comic in the Hebrew Bible*. Bible and Literature Series 23. JSOT Supplement Series 92. Sheffield, England: Almond Press, 1990.

Ruether, Rosemary Radford, ed. *Religion and Sexism*. New York: Simon & Schuster, 1974.

Russell, Letty M., ed. *Feminist Interpretation of the Bible*. Philadelphia: Westminster, 1985.

Sanders, James. *Canon and Community: A Guide to Canonical Criticism*. Guides to Biblical Scholarship. Old Testament Series. Philadelphia: Fortress Press, 1984.

Sugirtharajah, R. S., ed. *Voices from the Margin: Interpreting the Bible in the Third World*. Maryknoll, NY: Orbis, 1991.

Teubel, Savina J. *Hagar the Egyptian: The Lost Tradition of the Matriarchs*. San Francisco: Harper & Row, 1990.

———. *Sarah the Priestess*. Athens, OH: Swallow Press, 1984.

Trible, Phyllis. *God and the Rhetoric of Sexuality*. Overtures to Biblical Theology. Philadelphia: Fortress Press, 1978.

Weems, Renita J. *Just a Sister Away: A Womanist Vision of Women's Relationships in the Bible*. San Diego: LuraMedia, 1988.

Wegner, Judith Romney. *Chattel or Person? The Status of Women in the Mishnah*. New York: Oxford University Press, 1988.

Wilson, Robert R. *Prophecy and Society in Ancient Israel*. Philadelphia: Fortress Press, 1980.

Wren, Brian. *What Language Shall I Borrow? God-Talk in Worship: A Male Response to Feminist Theology*. New York: Crossroad, 1990.

Further Reading

This is a very brief selected bibliography consisting of works that you may find useful in preparing to teach *Biblical Women*. It is also appropriate for use by class participants who wish to continue to explore the methods introduced in this course in their reading of the Bible.

Reference Works

Anchor Bible Dictionary. Garden City, NY: Anchor/Doubleday, 1992.
This six-volume work is the best and most up-to-date Bible dictionary available. When you need further information on places, persons, and terms in biblical texts, it is an invaluable resource.

Achtemeier, Paul J., ed. *Harper's Bible Dictionary*. San Francisco: Harper & Row, 1985.
Harper's is a concise Bible dictionary, especially useful when *Anchor* is unavailable or too detailed.

Mays, James L., ed. *Harper's Bible Commentary*. San Francisco: Harper & Row, 1988.
A one-volume commentary that will provide background information on any book of the Bible and limited technical commentary. Also includes general articles.

Newsom, Carol, and Sharon H. Ringe, eds. *The Women's Bible Commentary*. Louisville, KY: Westminster/John Knox, 1992.
A new, valuable resource on women's scholarship and texts dealing with women in the Bible. Includes articles on every book of the Bible and a number of background articles.

Books on Women in the Bible, Women's Interpretation, and Related Topics

Christ, Carol P., and Judith Plaskow, eds. *Weaving the Visions: New Patterns in Feminist Spirituality*. San Francisco: HarperCollins, 1989.
An anthology of women's recent writings related to spirituality.

Falk, Marcia. *The Song of Songs: A New Translation and Interpretation.* San Francisco: HarperCollins, 1990.
A poet and scholar translates the Song of Songs into English poetry and offers commentary.

Fiorenza, Elisabeth Schüssler. *Bread Not Stone: The Challenge of Feminist Biblical Interpretation.* Boston: Beacon, 1985.
A feminist hermeneutic.

Fiorenza, Elisabeth Schüssler. *In Memory of Her: A Feminist Theological Reconstruction of Christian Origins.* New York: Crossroad/Continuum, 1983.
A feminist reconstruction of early Christianity. Valuable both for the specific information it provides and for the development of a feminist methodology.

Meyers, Carol. *Discovering Eve: Ancient Israelite Women in Context.* New York: Oxford University Press, 1988.
A biblical scholar and archaeologist, Meyers uses material remains and biblical texts to reconstruct the lives of early Israelite women.

Mollenkott, Virginia Ramey. *The Divine Feminine: The Biblical Imagery of God as Female.* New York: Crossroad, 1989.
An amazing resource on the range of feminine God-language in the Bible.

Proctor-Smith, Marjorie. *In Her Own Rite: Constructing Feminist Liturgical Tradition.* Nashville: Abingdon, 1990.
An evaluation and construction of liturgies that are grounded in both tradition and women's experience.

Trible, Phyllis. *God and the Rhetoric of Sexuality.* Overtures to Biblical Theology. Philadelphia: Fortress, 1978.
A positive feminist reclaiming of biblical texts and images.

Trible, Phyllis. *Texts of Terror: Literary-Feminist Readings of Biblical Narratives.* Philadelphia: Fortress, 1984.
A commemoration of women abused in the Bible.

Weems, Renita. *Just a Sister Away: A Womanist Vision of Women's Relationships in the Bible.* San Diego: LuraMedia, 1988.
An honest look at relationships among women in the Bible, and their counterparts today.

Wren, Brian. *What Language Shall I Borrow? God-Talk in Worship: A Male Response to Feminist Theology.* New York: Crossroad, 1990.
    A man enters into the quest for varied God-language. This is a book that has made some non-inclusive language fans reach for inclusion.

Biblical Women

Mirrors, Models, and Metaphors

Leader's Guide

Elizabeth Huwiler

A Kaleidoscope Series Resource

United Church Press
Cleveland, Ohio

Objectives of the Course

The course is designed so that each participant will:

1. Become increasingly aware of the roles available to women in Old and New Testament times

2. Become acquainted with a variety of stories about women from the Old and New Testaments

3. Practice applying various interpretive methods to biblical texts

4. Reflect on the significance of biblical stories and images for her or his own theology and prayer life

5. Become equipped to continue working with biblical texts in individual or group study

The Ideal Class Leader

This course is designed in a format that welcomes discussion and openness to various ideas and perspectives. Several of the interpretive methods invite participants to bring their own experiences and awareness of others into the class. The ideal leader will:

1. View herself or himself as an enabler, not as an answer provider

2. Be comfortable with silences in which participants are able to integrate material and reflect

3. Be aware that the Bible and gender relationships are issues about which people have strong feelings and beliefs, and be sensitive to personal responses and differences among class members

4. Be comfortable expressing his or her beliefs and experiences in a way that does not deny or denigrate those whose are different

5. Work at making the class a safe place for sharing responses to the material studied and relevant experiences, while at the same time recognizing that some participants may not be ready to share on every topic

6. Be aware when the class is developing an 'in-group' or 'party line' and make sure that no individual or group is silenced

7. Encourage the group to struggle with difficult issues

8. Respond to relevant interests and issues raised by the class, even if that means departing from the schedule in this Leader's Guide (but refer irrelevant issues to break or after-class discussion)

9. Prepare for leading the course by reading the entire book and viewing the entire video

10. Prepare for each class session by reviewing the chapter in the book, the Leader's Guide, and the video and making relevant preparations specific to the session

Leadership may be provided by one individual throughout the six sessions, by a team working together, or by different participants for different sessions.

Style of Class

Because the course deals with gender issues, the dynamics of the class may vary depending on whether the class is composed of women, men, or both, and depending on the variety of attitudes and experiences represented by the participants.

The course is designed for six two-hour sessions with one fifteen-minute break. Adaptation for a weekend retreat follows the instruction section for the six-session format. Other formats are possible, but it is recommended that there be twelve contact hours and additional time for preparation.

The ideal meeting place will permit flexible and informal seating. If possible, find a room that has chairs that can be arranged into a circle for whole-group discussion, turned toward a television for viewing the videotape, and moved into clusters for small-group discussion.

Have available newsprint (on an easel, if possible), markers, and masking tape (to mount newsprint on the walls).

Everyone should have a Bible at every class session. The course materials use the New Revised Standard Version. Although it is not necessary for everyone to use the same translation, translation differences may bog down the discussion if no one is able to explain their significance.

Learning will be more effective if participants share a commitment to the process. Encourage group members to agree to be faithful in attendance and diligent in preparation. While it is important to encourage a safe atmosphere for sharing personal experiences, feelings, and beliefs, it is also important to respect participants' need to keep some parts of themselves private. An ideal setting will allow participants to feel welcome but not pushed to share themselves with the group.

The Bible is a valuable resource, not only for study but also for worship and meditation. Encourage the group to discuss the desirability of opening and closing devotions or meditations. These devotions and meditations may be led by different individuals or groups at different class sessions.

Small groups (with a maximum of four participants) are important to the learning process. The same groups may work together throughout the six sessions, or the makeup of the groups may vary from one session to the next. (Continuing groups have the advantage of developing trust and a group identity, but a member who does not fit into a group risks being distressed for the entire course or even dropping out.) I recommend that this decision be negotiated as part of the initial commitment the class makes to the course.

Several of the sessions (chapters 3, 4, and 5) produce materials to display on the walls or on tables. If others who use the room are agreeable, leave these on display to provide continuity from week to week. If they cannot be left out between sessions, consider saving them and displaying them in subsequent weeks.

Chapter One: Women's Roles
Historical Reconstruction

Objectives

1. To create an atmosphere in which participants will feel open to learn and explore

2. To come to an understanding about participants' commitment to the course and to one another

3. To reflect on the relationship between women's experience and historical records

4. To become aware of the range of women's roles in biblical times

Materials

Newsprint, markers, masking tape
A Bible for each participant
TV and VCR

Class Session
1. Ice-breaker (10 minutes). Have each participant introduce herself or himself. Ask participants to share events that defines their roles in family or community.
2. Present an overview of the course (20 minutes). Show video segment 1A (introduction to course). At the end of the segment, stop the tape and:
   a. On newsprint, list the course objectives
   b. Explain the learning style
   c. Invite the participants to commit to shared goals (attendance; preparation; openness with respect for privacy; devotions or not—and if so, leadership; small groups—permanent or changing).
3. Women in history (25 minutes). Divide the class into small groups of not more than four people. Ask them to discuss the following questions. How does available history reflect or neglect my life or that of women close to me? What would history books have to include in order to take account of women's lives? What would have to be added to history books in order for future generations to understand what it is like to be a woman today?

Reassemble the entire group. Invite a representative from each small group to report the substance of their discussion. Suggest that what "counts" in history books may differ from what women count as important in their lives. Invite participants to reflect on what has been important to them compared with what makes newspaper headlines.
4. Break (15 minutes).
5. Reconstructing the past as a method (10 minutes). Explain that artifacts are important in helping historians to reconstruct the past. To prepare for video segment 1B, ask participants to note the areas of life that are suggested by different artifacts. Show video segment 1B.
6. The lives of women in biblical times (20 minutes). In small groups, ask students to reflect on the material in chapter 1. Was any of the information in this chapter a surprise? How does the information here change, challenge, or confirm your ideas about biblical women? Will it make a difference as you read other biblical texts? What do you hope will happen as you progress through the course?
7. Return to large group. Invite representative from each small group to summarize the responses to chapter 1 and hopes for course.

8. Closing (10 minutes). Invite participants to formulate their hopes for course into one-sentence blessings (e.g., "May we learn from the lives of women in the Bible; may we grow in awareness of God's will for us").

Assignment for the Next Session

Ask each group member to choose the character from chapter 2 with whom she or he identifies most readily and the one who is the most difficult to understand.

Chapter Two: Women and Women Dynamic Analogy

Objectives

1. To think about the ways women relate to other women in biblical times and today

2. To practice identifying with a variety of biblical women

3. To become aware of parallels between relationships among biblical characters and relationships among women today

Materials

Newsprint, markers, masking tape

A Bible for each participant

Advance Preparation

Arrange chairs in circle

Class Session

1. Issues (15 minutes). Invite participants to raise issues from the assigned chapter that they wish to discuss. Write these issues on newsprint. Decide which are best addressed at the outset and which will fit more readily into a later segment of the class. Invite large group to raise issues related to dynamic analogy as a method; ask group to respond to issues.

2. Small group discussion (25 minutes). Invite groups to share among themselves the characters they chose as easiest to identify with and most difficult to understand. Ask participants to tell each other what made identification easy or challenging.

3. Reassemble in large group (15 minutes). Introduce video segment 2 (small group of women and men doing dynamic analogy). Ask participants to note how the method worked and to use the video group as a model for their own discussion. Show the video segment. Allow time for reactions.

4. Break (15 minutes)

5. Small groups (30 minutes). Assign each group one of the texts from the chapter, and assign each group member one of the roles within the text. Have each participant (1) tell the story to the small groups from the point of view of her/his character, and (2) discuss differing perceptions of the story from the different characters' points of view. It is all right for participants to disagree about how a character would perceive the story. The aim of this exercise is not to come up with a right answer but to explore possibilities. Emphasize that group members are not to censor each other. One person in each group can be recorder for the group, writing down important learnings from using this method.

6. Summary (10 minutes). Return to large group. Write group summaries on newsprint.

7. As a closing devotion (10 minutes), go around the circle and have each member offer a thanksgiving or blessing related to the character with whom he or she identified.

Assignment for Next Session

Ask participants to clip advertisements that show women and men interacting.

Chapter 3: Women and Men
Hermeneutic of Suspicion

Objectives

1. To think about the ways women relate to men now and in biblical times

2. To learn to ask suspicious questions about the way relationships are represented

3. To practice filling in the gaps in biblical texts

Materials
    Construction paper, glue
    Newsprint, markers, masking tape
    A Bible for each participant

Note: Suspicion can be a difficult, even threatening, method when people first attempt to apply it to biblical texts. Stress the importance of not judging each other.

Class Session
    1. Invite participants to paste their ad cutouts to poster board (10 minutes).

    2. Suspicion (20 minutes). Introduce video segment 3A. The segment illustrates suspicious questions to ask of an advertisement. As participants watch the segment, they should note the questions and try to learn how to ask similarly suspicious questions. Show the video segment. Stop the video. Ask participants to look at the ad cutouts. What do the advertisements suggest about the ways women and men relate to each other? Are they at all suspicious of the suggestions? Whose interests are being served? (It is likely that some advertisements will be overtly sexist while others may have an overtly feminist message.) Invite participants to write suspicious questions on the poster board around the advertisements.

    3. Large group discussion (20 minutes). Can they ask similar suspicious questions of biblical texts? This is a time to emphasize the class as a safe place for exploring unfamiliar ideas. Observe that this is a difficult method for people who have been taught to trust the text and submit to it. Is it possible to do both? Can one honor the text through questioning it? (Some participants may latch onto this method as liberating while other may find it threatening. Try to help them to hear one another without judging.)

    4. Break (15 minutes).

    5. Suspicion in action (20 minutes). Introduce video segment 3B. This is a group trying to practice a hermeneutic of suspicion on texts from this chapter. Note that the participants in the tape have difficulty sticking to the method. Ask group members to identify when the people in the tape are moving away from suspicion.

    6. Divide into small groups to practice suspicion (20 minutes). Ask participants to try suspicion on Numbers 12. Suggest that one

volunteer in each small group read the text. How convincing was the analysis in the textbook? Do they have additional suspicions? What parallel story might support Miriam's interests?

7. Large group summary and closing (15 minutes). What did the small groups learn? Summarize on newsprint. Close by inviting benedictions for Miriam.

Assignment for Next Session

Find magazine pictures that illustrate women who are "the least" in our culture.

Chapter 4: Women and Jesus
Reading from Below

Objectives

1. To analyze the ways women in Gospel stories relate to Jesus
2. To consider the different ways participants can relate to Jesus in their own faith lives
3. To try identifying with "the least" character in a text

Materials

Poster board, paste
Newsprint, markers, masking tape
A Bible for each participant

Advance Preparation

Practice leading the guided meditation in paragraph 2 under "Class Session." Allow time for reflection where there are ellipses in the text. The time needed for the meditation will vary according to whether participants are accustomed to contemplative exercises. As you lead, watch for signs that they are relaxed and ready to move to the next element.

Class Session

1. In small groups, paste magazine pictures to construction paper or poster board (10 minutes; each group combines its pictures on a single board).
2. Guided meditation (20 minutes). Invite participants to find a

comfortable position, relax, close their eyes. Allow a minute or so of silence, then read Mark 5:25–34. After reading the passage once, invite participants to imagine themselves as the woman:

You have been bleeding for twelve years. You have been ritually unclean for twelve years, unable to enter the temple. Jesus is in town. You are making your way to the place where Jesus is, pushing your way through the crowd. . . . If you can touch his clothes, you will be well. You are getting closer to Jesus. You can reach his cloak. You touch it. . . . You feel the bleeding stop. You are well. . . . Jesus stops. Are you afraid of what he will say? . . . "Who touched my clothes?" How do you feel? . . . You hear the disciples. You see him still looking around. You are afraid. . . . You make your way to Jesus, you fall down before him, you tell him your story. . . . He is about to speak to you. . . . "Daughter, your faith has made you well; go in peace, and be healed." (Allow another minute or so of silence.)

What is your hidden illness? What is it that would make them think you unclean if they knew? How long have you suffered silently? . . . Make your way to Jesus. . . . You are pressing through the crowd . . . Now you are near enough to touch him . . . When you touch him, you are healed. Feel the healing as it flows through your body. . . . Jesus stops. What will he say? . . . "Who touched my clothes?" Can you admit that it was you? . . . The disciples speak; Jesus is still looking around. . . . You are afraid. You have touched the holy one while you were unclean. . . . Kneel before him now. Tell Jesus your story, your illness and the healing you have experienced. . . . "Daughter, your faith has made you well; go in peace, and be healed."

(Allow another minute or so of silence; then invite participants to return to the class.)

3. Small group discussion (20 minutes). Invite participants to share what they wish of the experience. How did it feel to touch Jesus? What was the healing like?

4. Break (15 minutes).

5. Large group (25 minutes). Introduce video segment 4, a conversation with two women who minister in women's shelters. Invite participants to listen for references to "the least" in the discussion. Show video segment. Invite responses.

6. Small groups (20 minutes). Return to discussion of Mark 5:25–34 and photos brought to class. How do the characters in the clippings correspond to the woman with the hidden illness? How

might they experience Jesus' healing? Imagine a message of healing from Jesus to one of the women, and imagine her response. Write these messages on the poster board.

7. Closing devotion (10 minutes). Invite participants to share their understanding of Jesus' message of healing and the woman's response. After each shared understandings, the group is invited to respond with "Amen."

Chapter Five: Women in the Garden
Interpreting the Tradition

Objectives

1. To develop awareness of how our readings of the Eden story and the Song of Songs have been affected by their interpretive history

2. To explore new readings of the stories of Eden and the Song of Songs

3. To express our own sense of woman in the garden

4. To explore positive images of sexuality for the church

Materials

Newsprint, markers, masking tape
A Bible for each participant
Paper, marking pens, clay
Tables to work at

Class Session

1. Large group (15 minutes). Summarize. The traditional interpretation of the Eden story has been very influential in our understanding of women and the relationships between men and women. This traditional interpretation has been effected through both interpretive studies and artistic expressions. The video segment will show some of the artistic slant on the Eden story. Show video segment.

2. Small group discussion (25 minutes). What does this say about the way the church and Western society have understood women in the garden? How have you personally experienced the Eden story?

3. Break (15 minutes).

4. Large group (20 minutes). Respond to new readings of Eden story and Song of Songs as presented in the reading for this week. What was surprising? What did you find yourself resisting?

5. Small group or individual time (35 minutes). Play with paper and marking pens or with clay to express your own feelings about or understanding of women in the garden. Display results. Allow time for questions and comments.

6. Closing blessing (10 minutes). Each participant chooses another's artistic statement and makes a blessing or thanksgiving about one aspect of it.

Chapter Six: Gender and God
Constructive Biblical Theology

Objectives

1. To develop awareness of the variety of images in the Bible that refer to God

2. To develop awareness of the power of language

3. To explore different ways of speaking about God in private devotion and public worship

4. To contemplate continued study of the Bible according to methods learned in this class

Materials

Newsprint, markers, masking tape
A Bible for each participant
Worship resources (contemporary hymnals, prayer collections, etc.)
Paper, pens or pencils
Tables for groups to work at

Note: It's possible that participants will be offended by each other's ideas. Some may not be open to traditional language, and others may have a hard time talking about God in non-traditional terms.

Class Session

1. Large group (30 minutes). Summarize. Worship language is powerful and personal. As you watch and listen to the video segment,

note your personal reactions. How does it feel to hear this language used in worship? Can you worship this way? Can you be at home in a congregation that worships this way? Show the segment (people reading blessings, prayers, etc). Allow safe space for class members to express responses. Urge class members to respect one another's responses. We are different but does that mean we can't worship together? (If all class members agree on general response, ask whether we are open to worshiping with others who do not respond the same way we do.)

2. Large group (10 minutes). Highlight the issues of the chapter. Note that there may be too much here to absorb in one reading; that's all right. Suggest that participants try to come back to these issues on their own.

3. Large group (10 minutes). Introduce the idea of producing a brief liturgy to close the course. This is a way of experiencing the issues raised in this chapter. Assign different portions (call to worship, prayer, song, litany, commissioning and benediction) to different small groups. If group members are not able or willing to worship together in an experimental liturgy, individuals or groups may develop liturgical segments to present for discussion rather than worship.

4. Break (15 minutes).

5. Small groups (25 minutes). Each group works on its own segment. Unless you have access to a photocopier, the parts to be read by large group should be written clearly on newsprint and posted where all participants can see them.

6. Large group (10 minutes). What happens after the class is over? Show video segment 6B.

7. Large group (20 minutes). Celebrate the liturgy together.

Adapting the Course for a Weekend Retreat (Friday Evening through Sunday Morning)

This course is well-suited for a weekend study retreat. Participants should agree to read the entire book before the start of the retreat. Invite them to bring either an advertisement featuring male-female interaction or a photograph of a woman who represents "the least" (see preparation for chapters 3 and 4 in this Leader's

Guide). If you are working with a small group, you might also invite each participant to select a chapter and help lead that class session. Be sure to take with you all necessary materials for all class sessions, and be sure that you have access to a TV and VCR.

Friday evening. Gathering and introductions. Follow chapter 1 as outlined. Close with song.

Saturday 8:30-11:00 A.M. Follow guidelines for chapter 2; after a brief break, continue with the first part of chapter 3 (until break). If possible, allow an opportunity for outdoor exercise before lunch.

Saturday 1:00-4:00 P.M. Resume with the remainder of chapter 3, a brief break, and all of chapter 4. Try to arrange an opportunity for outdoor exercise at the end of the session.

Saturday 7:00-9:00 P.M. Follow guidelines for chapter 5. The session could be followed by a casual fellowship period.

Sunday 8:00-9:00 A.M. Follow guidelines for chapter 6 until the break, adding the final video segment. Ask participants to prepare a full service of worship.

Sunday 9:15-10:15 A.M. Small groups meet separately to prepare their parts of the worship.

Sunday 10:30 A.M. Entire group gathers for closing worship.